"Vance Havner used the Word of God like a sword. You pick any one of his books and you could sense the presence and power of the Holy Spirit leaping off those pages."

—BILLY GRAHAM

"What a privilege it was to know Vance Havner and to hear him preach the Word! He is imitated but he will never be duplicated. I rejoice that we have his ministry available to a new generation that is seeking something more than 'the average Christian life.'"

—WARREN W. WIERSBE
Author and Conference Speaker

"All of us have quoted Vance Havner, but now in this book we get to read his sermons, always pithy, ever relevant and most assuredly convicting. Those who are acquainted with Havner will be eager to read these messages. Those introduced to him for the first time will have gained a wonderful friend."

—ERWIN LUTZER
Moody Church

"Dr. Vance Havner was a prophet of righteousness and revival. His diagnosis of the world and church conditions revealed a supernatural discernment that astounded audiences. But more importantly, his biblical prescriptions and prophetic preaching always provided the Divine remedy."

—STEPHEN F. OLFORD
Founder and Chairman of Olford Ministries International
and Senior Lecturer at the Stephen Olford Center
for Biblical Preaching, Memphis, Tennessee

"I knew Vance Havner for several decades. He loved pastors and they loved him. I . . . pray that the new generations of preachers who did not have the privilege of knowing him would read *When God Breaks Through* and catch his spirit. Their lives will be forever enriched as they do."

—JAMES DRAPER
President of LifeWay Christian Resources

"You owe it to yourself to buy this book and any other book of Havner's you can find."

—MICHAEL CATT
Pastor, Sherwood Baptist Church, Albany, Georgia
www.2prophetU.com

"Vance Havner was one of a kind. His bold proclamation, unique wordplay and homespun stories combined to encourage and inspire those who heard him. It is a joy to know that a new generation of preachers and church leaders will benefit from Havner's preaching through this outstanding collection of revival sermons."

—MICHAEL DUDUIT
Editor, *Preaching* magazine
www.Preaching.com

"Vance Havner had one of the best pens around. His unique way of expressing time-honored truths was always significant and Spirit blessed. Anyone who reads Havner is in store for a rich blessing."

—LEWIS A. DRUMMOND
Professor of Evangelism in residence at the Billy Graham Evangelism Training Center at the Cove and Chancellor of the Schools of Evangelism of the Billy Graham Evangelistic Association

"Vance Havner painted poignant word pictures the reader just doesn't forget. Reading Havner always provides fresh insight and understanding about the Christian Life. Havner never pulled punches or wasted words, but insightfully cut right to the point."

—BOB DASAL
Editor-in-Chief, *Pulpit Helps* magazine

"The last century produced no greater revivalist than Vance Havner. His grasp of what is necessary to position ourselves for a moving of God's Spirit is legendary. This is a fresh new series including many of Havner's sermons published for the first time. It is a book bound to encourage, challenge and, ultimately, bless you."

—TOM ELLIFF
Pastor, First Southern Baptist Church
Del City, Oklahoma

WHEN GOD
BREAKS THROUGH

VANCE HAVNER

WHEN GOD BREAKS THROUGH

Sermons on Revival

Edited and compiled by
Dennis J. Hester

Kregel
Publications

When God Breaks Through: Sermons on Revival by Vance Havner

© 2003 by Dennis J. Hester, editor and compiler

Published by Kregel Publications, a division of Kregel, Inc., P.O. Box 2607, Grand Rapids, MI 49501.

Scripture quotations are from the King James Version of the Holy Bible.

Library of Congress Cataloging-in-Publication Data
Havner, Vance
When God breaks through: sermons on revival / by Vance Havner; edited and compiled by Dennis Hester.
       p. cm.
    1. Evangelical sermons. 2. Baptists—Sermons.
3. Sermons, American—20th Century. I. Hester, Dennis J.
II. Title.
BV3797.H43W48   2003
252'.3—dc21   2003012164

ISBN 978-0-8254-2873-9

Printed in the United States of America

14 15 / 7 6 5 4

CONTENTS

A TRIBUTE TO VANCE HAVNER

*B*illy Graham calls Vance Havner the most quoted preacher in America, adding that no one has done more to fan the flames of revival than has Vance Havner. Havner was already a popular speaker at Bible conferences when Graham first met him at Florida Bible Institute (now Trinity College), where Havner was speaking. As a boy, Graham read an inspirational column that Havner wrote for the *Charlotte* (North Carolina) *Observer,* Graham's hometown.

When I was a young preacher and would-be writer, Havner reviewed some of my inspirational newspaper columns. He said, "I would keep this up and make it a priority, if I were you. I would not make it *the* priority, but I would make it a priority." He added, "If what you say has value, it will last longer than you will." That was prophetic of Vance Havner's life and ministry.

Even though he has been in heaven since August 12, 1986, his recorded sermons still are aired on radio, and his printed sermons are read even in cyberspace. Born in 1901 in the rural community of Vale, outside of Hickory, North Carolina, Havner lived from the era of horse-drawn buggies into the jet age, dying at age eighty-five.

Years ago Havner told about a visitor to Spurgeon's

famous Tabernacle in London. The visitor asked a church member the difference between Spurgeon and other preachers. The member said, "Well, when other preachers preached it was good. But when Mr. Spurgeon preached, there was fire."

Many people feel the same way about Havner. He was a prince among preachers, a clever wordsmith, and an anointed man of God who preached with boldness, clarity, and conviction. He was true to God's Word and used it as a flaming sword to pierce the hearts of sinners and saints alike. Havner said, "I've never known a time that I didn't feel called to preach." He had few hobbies or special interests other than preaching. He didn't travel the world or take exotic vacations. He studied; he read; he wrote newspaper columns; he wrote articles for various religious magazines; he penned over thirty books of devotions and sermons.

Havner married late in life and had no children. For over seven decades Havner made a tremendous sacrifice by committing himself to what he was called to do and what he did best—preaching the gospel and writing books. He was small in stature and spoke with a bit of a nasal twang. He often looked a bit frail and did not demand attention when he stepped behind the pulpit. But when he preached, people could tell that he had been with Jesus. He was truly an instrument in God's hands. He spoke with purpose and power, and the Holy Spirit used him to touch the raw nerves in listeners' hearts. On many occasions he reminded his audience of the old aphorism, "I have come to comfort the afflicted and afflict the comfortable." Havner knew nothing of being politically correct. He told it like it was and let the chips fall where they might. He preached on topics that some today find outdated—heaven, hell, sin, repentance, sacrifice, holiness, revival, prayer, and the lordship of Christ. Havner said, "Jesus will be Lord of all or He will not be Lord at all."

"You can't tell it like it is, if you don't believe it like it was," said Havner, as he addressed the student body of Gardner-Webb College (now University) in 1974. That was the first time I heard him preach. I wrote this memorable quote in the front of my Bible, and I've been reading and sharing his priceless wit and practical wisdom ever since.

They say of old preachers, "The old fellows are gone, but not forgotten." Havner added, "And the trouble with us preachers today is, we're forgotten, but not gone."

Havner in many ways reminded me of Elijah, a prophet who spoke a fresh and convicting word that was often uncomfortable as well as liberating. And like Elijah, Havner was a holy man of God, "passing by." To be holy, we must spend time with a holy God, and that was one of Havner's daily habits, spending time with God. Havner said, "If we don't 'come a-part' and spend time with God, we will 'come apart' emotionally and spiritually."

Havner was a bird watcher and spent hours watching, listening, and learning about birds and their habits. This pastime allowed him to walk for exercise and afforded him the solitude he needed for prayer and meditation. A mystic, marching to the beat of a different drummer, he lived and ministered on a different level from most ministers.

Graham described Havner this way: "Someone has said everyone is born an original and dies a copy. That wasn't true of Vance Havner. Vance Havner was born an original, and he died an original" (from Havner's funeral message delivered by Graham at Havner's home church, First Baptist Church of Greensboro, North Carolina).

Havner didn't care to be "one of the boys," nor did he want

to be the center of attention or the class clown. He was some-
what of a loner, and his desire to live on a higher spiritual
level, untangled from the trappings of success and material-
ism, may have caused him to appear peculiar and unsociable.
But those who knew him best knew he had a tender heart and
a gentle spirit. Waiting, reflecting, watching, and listening for
that "still small voice"—that was Vance Havner.

Like the prophet Micaiah, Havner was lonely, speaking for
God regardless of the consequences (1 Kings 22:7–8). He did
not have a circle of friends that he depended upon to make
things happen for him. No brochures, no radio or television
advertisements, and no evangelistic organization promoted
his speaking ministry. Still, he never lacked for a place to
preach.

He traveled alone, until at age forty he married Sara Allred.
Havner never had a driver's license, but he finally bought a
car when he was sixty. Not being one to make hasty decisions,
Havner said, concerning these types of important decisions,
"I wanted to think it over a bit." Sara became his chauffeur
and constant companion. He said, "Sara drove, and I prayed."

Even in Havner's late sixties, he often preached weeks at a
time without a break and continued to preach until he went
to be with the Lord. He often told his audiences, "When I
get a little older, I'm going to have to slow down." He once
said, "Last week I was introduced at a preaching conference
as being 'retired.' Boy, you should have heard me when I
stepped up to the pulpit. I told them. 'I've been preaching
for three weeks straight without a break, and I come here to
preach and find out that I'm retired. I am "tired," but I'm
not "retired."'"

Seeing pastors fail to make time with God a priority, Havner
called ministers to a lifestyle of solitude, meditation, and

reflection. One of his favorite sermon themes was "the out-living of the in-living Christ." To do so takes an intimate and consistent relationship with our Lord, and it was always evident that Havner had "been with Jesus."

"What we need," said Havner, "is preachers who will take their Bibles and spend some time in the woods alone with God. And then they would come out of the woods a new man." Havner understood, of course, that merely going to the woods was not the key to obtaining a spirit-filled and holy life. He said, "The monks tried to be holy by living in caves. But you can't be holy by hiding in a hole. It takes time talking to God and listening to God. We don't need more Bible study as much as we need reflecting on what we already know that's in the Bible. We need to take the time to just think about the things of God."

Havner kept his focus on both Jesus and his own calling to be a preacher. Once he was asked, "How do you want to be remembered?" He said, "I want to be remembered as 'just a preacher.' Any more would be too much and any less would be unnecessary." He was humbled and felt honored to be cho-sen as one of God's spokesmen.

Havner did not graduate from high school, college, or semi-nary. He attended Wake Forest College, Catawba College, and Moody Bible Institute but did not graduate from any of these schools. One of his teachers at Boiling Springs High School (now Gardner-Webb University) gave the young Havner some unconventional advice: "Vance, if I were you, I believe I would blaze my own trail." No doubt this wise teacher saw the hand of God upon this young preacher boy, and the advice offered by that teacher apparently took root; Havner wasn't a rebel nor a radical, but an iconoclast. He bucked tradition and min-istered as he felt led of God.

Havner served two churches as a pastor: Salem Baptist Church in Weeksville, North Carolina, where he served at two different times; and the First Baptist Church of Charleston, South Carolina, for five years, beginning in 1934. Havner, however, did not have a pastor's heart. He delegated much of his responsibilities for funerals and weddings to his associate pastor and detested business conferences and administration. His heart was in preaching, and in 1939 he went into full-time evangelism. Havner preferred to be called a "revivalist" or "exhorter," to being known as an "evangelist."

Havner kept his focus ever on Jesus. He said in his second devotional book, *Consider Jesus* (1939), "The Bible is important, but it is only God's Word about Christ. The Spirit is important, but He testifies only of Christ. Doctrine is important, but a doctrine is just a truth about Christ. Experience is important, but an experience is just another step with Christ." Is it any wonder that Havner would write a book entitled *Jesus Only*?

This collection of Havner's messages reveals that he preached the gospel with a sense of urgency. As Richard Baxter suggested in *Love Breathing Thanks and Praise,* Havner preached "as never sure to preach again, and as a dying man to dying men." Havner challenged preachers to enter the pulpit as though for the first time, as though it could be the best time, and as though it might be the last time. And he emphasized that the preacher needed to love the people he was preaching to as much as he loved preaching.

Havner knew that people were lost and hopeless without Christ. That's why he challenged and sometimes "lambasted" the church when it took lightly its responsibility of proclaiming the gospel and witnessing to the truth.

Never losing his passion for lost souls, Havner often said,

"We've been called out of this world to go back into the world to call others out of this world, and that's all the business we've got in this world." Havner determined preaching and calling his listeners to make a public decision for Christ a high priority. And the next step—discipleship—was of equal importance. Havner often quoted a Christian motto that was transformed from a dye factory motto: "We live to dye and dye to live. The more we dye the more we live. And the more we live, the more we dye." He used this illustration to call Christians back to a commitment to God.

Havner's homespun style of storytelling and word play often left his listeners laughing, enlightened, and conflicted. Although not mean-spirited in his preaching or witnessing, Havner sometimes was criticized for being too negative or too hard on preachers and other church leaders. He unashamedly reminded his listeners, "Sometimes you hear congregations say concerning a preacher's message, 'I didn't get it.' It's not our place that they get it; it's our place to see that they hear it."

If ever we need to see a "holy man of God passing by," it is today. Havner's Bible-centered messages of revival will be forever relevant, because the human heart is forever the same. As Havner says, "Nothing of importance has changed."

I pray that these timeless messages from Havner will warm your heart, challenge your soul, and will bring you to that holy place "when God breaks through with genuine revival."

ACKNOWLEDGMENTS

Thanks are extended to my friend Anita Barrett for her diligence in helping to transcribe Havner's messages.

Thanks go to the fine people at Kregel Publications, especially to Dennis Hillman, publisher, for his vision for Havner's sermons and for the opportunity to compile and edit these sermons by my favorite preacher.

In collections such as this, discrepancies sometimes exist between the spoken word of those who preach and the written word of those who transcribe those sermons. As much as possible, these printed messages are as Havner spoke them. But, as compiler and editor, I have taken the liberty of clarifying and shortening long introductions and invitations, and deleting illustrations and examples that Havner repeated in other messages.

The sermon "Amos: The Prophet with a Modern Message for America" was previously published by Zondervan Publishing Company as "Amos: The Prophet with a Modern Message" and is used here by permission.

Chapter 1

WHEN GOD
BREAKS THROUGH

*L*isten to the voice of the prophet Isaiah pleading for divine visitation: "Oh that thou wouldest rend the heavens, that thou wouldest come down, that the mountains might flow down at thy presence" (Isa. 64:1). Isaiah was a faithful preacher during a time when his nation was going to pieces. The people were trying to stave off disaster by alliance here and there, but Isaiah stood his ground and declared that all their schemes would crack up in defeat unless they turned to God. The prophet looked around at the condition of the country and then looked back to remember the days of old. He said, "When thou didst terrible things which we looked not for, thou camest down, the mountains flowed down at thy presence" (Isa. 64:3).

God's manifestations at Sinai with Moses, Joshua, Gideon, and David were when Israel walked in power. The prophet says in effect, "Lord, do it again." He uses three reasons in telling the people why God is *not* coming down in power. These same reasons hold true today.

The first reason is our sins. God is not visiting us in revival today because we are still rebelling. Rarely do you hear people say, as David did, "Against thee, only, have I sinned" (Ps. 51:4). I used to wonder why David said that. I thought he had sinned against just about everybody, including Uriah, Bathsheba, the nation, and himself. But David had a proper concept of sin. He regarded sin first and foremost as something against God. We don't hear people say that today. We need to face, first of all, our own sins as Christians. "To him that knoweth to do good, and doeth it not, to him it is sin" (James 4:17). That should be enough to put us on our knees. There are sins of omission, sins of commission, sins of disposition, and sins of doubtful things—not just our mistakes, not just our blunders, not just our imperfection, but our sins. We have not only our sinful natures, but also our sinful deeds. God is not breaking through because we have sinned and have not repented.

The second reason why God is not breaking through is that we are an unclean thing: "All our righteousnesses are as filthy rags" (Isa. 64:6). Our sins and self-made righteousness are less than nothing. The Bible says our righteousness is as filthy rags, because they don't cover us, and filthy because they only defile us. We have so much self-righteousness that we are too good to have a revival. The Laodiceans were in that same awful state. They were rich and increased with goods; they had need of nothing. But all that good is not enough. Our Lord said, "Except your righteousness exceed that of the scribes and the Pharisees, ye shall in no wise enter into the kingdom of heaven" (Matt. 5:20). But how good were they? I believe they were plenty good. Do you know what a church full of Pharisees today would be like? Everybody would go to church; everybody would read the Bible; everybody would pray in public; everybody would be separated; everybody would give a tithe; everybody would try to win other folks to their belief; and everybody would be lost! That's how good you can be and not be good enough. We need another kind of righteousness. This other righteousness is the implanted, the imported, and the imputed righteousness of Christ.

I'm especially concerned about the third reason why God isn't visiting us today with a great manifestation of His power. Notice Isaiah 64:7: "There is none that calleth upon thy name, that stirreth up himself to take hold of thee." Telescope that statement a little bit and you have this: "There is none that stirreth up himself to take hold of God." We're living today in a tired age. Everybody is tired. I'm glad the Lord fails not, neither is weary, because everybody else today is tuckered out. Look at all of our laborsaving devices. Our grandmothers could bring up a dozen children and still have time to pray and read the Bible, but by the time you've turned on and turned off these laborsaving gadgets for a whole day, you're a wreck. We go to bed tired. We get up tired—physically, mentally, spiritually. It seems a deep sleep has descended upon us and the Devil has chloroformed the atmosphere.

It seems we are walking in our sleep. We go through all the motions, but sometimes church work is just glorified self-exaltation. No wonder the Bible says, "Awake thou that sleepest, arise from the dead, and Christ shall give thee light" (Eph. 5:14). "Awake to righteousness, and sin not; for some have not the knowledge of God: I speak this to your shame" (1 Cor. 15:34). Our Lord said in the garden, "Sleep on now" (Matt. 26:45). A lot of folks today are obeying just that much of what He said. They're still sleeping. But the next thing He said was, "Rise, let us be going" (Matt. 26:46). It says in Isaiah, "There is none that stirreth up himself to take hold of God" (64:7). Notice that it doesn't say, "There is none that stirreth up himself," period. There has never been a time when the church was stirring up itself more than it is now. We've never had more rattlesnakes than we have now. But so much of all this activity does not get hold of God. We read the Bible, we pray, we go to church, and these things are a means to an end. So often, however, they stop right there. Our Lord's accusation at Sardis was simply this: "I have not found thy works perfect before God [fulfilled in the sight of God]" (Rev. 3:2). Oh, they were doing a lot of good things, and they were as busy as could be. They were doing more and more, however, of less and less. These people were not getting through to God.

A lot of dear folks today are either in a state of cholera morbus or St. Vitus's dance [the twitching nerve disorder chorea]. We need to get going for God. Faith in itself has no value unless it connects you with God. The Bible is constantly trying to wake us up: "Stir up the gift of God" (2 Tim. 1:6); "Break up your fallow ground" (Hos. 10:12); "Gird up the loins of your mind" (1 Peter 1:13). We need to take ourselves by the nape of the neck and make ourselves do what we know we ought to do, whether we feel like it or not.

Some time ago I woke up in the middle of the night. The weather had changed and I was cold. There was a warm blanket at the foot of the bed, but I was so sleepy I didn't get myself together and apply the remedy. I went around with a "crick" in my neck for several days. A lot of people know why God isn't breaking through today; they know where the remedy is, but they never stir up themselves to take hold of God. Some people are waiting for a lovely feeling to come. Sam Jones used to say, "If I went out to chop wood and you found me out there sitting with my axe on my knees, and not a chip in sight, you could reasonably ask, 'What are you waiting for?' What would you think if I said, 'Well, I'm waiting until I work up a sweat. When I do that, I want to chop wood.'"

A lot of dear people are waiting for a lovely feeling. You have a Bible there. Read it. Pray whether you feel like it or not.

Go to God's house to pray. March yourself to the place "where prayer is wont to be made." Get one foot in front of the other and walk down that church aisle and do the thing you ought to do. "There is none that stirreth up himself to take hold of God" (Isa. 64:7)—that's what hinders the visitation of God in the church today. Our sinfulness, our self-righteousness, and our sluggishness hinder the ministry of the Spirit. Whatever your trouble is, apply the means of grace and do something about it. God will visit you. God will break through again.

Chapter 2

REVIVE US AGAIN

*N*otice in 2 Chronicles 7:13–14 that each part of these verses starts with *if.* "If I shut up heaven that there be no rain, or if I command the locusts to devour the land, or if I send pestilence among my people . . ." Then there's one more *if,* the remedy to the misfortunes: "If my people. . . ." Notice how the focus here and in the following verses swings back and forth, how it oscillates between God and His people. The passage is remarkable.

> If my people, which are called by my name, shall humble themselves, and pray, and seek my face, and turn from their wicked ways; then will I hear from heaven, and will forgive their sin, and will heal their land. (2 Chron. 7:14)

Here we have God's prescription for an awakening. When I announce this text I'm aware that some of the saints settle back in the pews as if to say, "Well, I've heard all this before." But one of our great needs today is to familiarize ourselves with the familiar, to get better acquainted with what we already know.

We sing "Revive Us Again." Sometimes I have an uneasy feeling that when we sing "Revive Us Again," we add under our breath, "But not now." And I think it's rankest hypocrisy to ask God to revive us again if we won't do the four things that He says in this passage, "If my people. . . ."

God begins with His people, and His people begin with themselves. This old Bible is a very personal book. "Search me and know my heart. Try me and know my faults. See if there be any wicked way in me, and lead me in the way everlasting" (see Ps. 139:23–24). Whoever prayed that was not passing the buck. This is personal, you notice. When David committed his terrible sin, he needed to do something besides grab a harp and start singing songs. And he got down to business. "Against thee, thee only, have I sinned" (Ps. 51:4). I used to wonder why he had said that. I thought he had sinned against just about everybody—you or I, Bathsheba, himself, and the whole country. But he realized that sin was between him and God. And when people pray like that, the Holy Spirit has been at work. You hear plenty of people say, "Oh, I know I'm not as good as I ought to be," and "I'm my own worst enemy," and trivial things like that. They are nowhere near conviction. But when the Holy Spirit plays upon the heartstrings, a person is likely to say, "Oh God, against Thee and Thee only have I sinned."

We sometimes sing "Lord, send a revival, and let it begin in me," or we sing with the old spiritual, "Not the preacher, nor the deacon, but it's me, Oh Lord, standing in the need of prayer." Those are good words to sing. You know, it doesn't take much religion to confess other people's sins. Some people are mighty good at that. A woman went to a psychiatrist, and she had a strip of bacon over each ear and a fried egg on top of her head. She said, "I've come to see you about my brother." She needed a little help herself. Did you ever hear somebody in a prayer meeting take a trip around the world and visit all of the mission fields, and you felt like saying, "Brother, if I were you, I'd back up and start over with myself." That's a good place to start.

Notice our text talks about the "people that are called by my name." You say, "What's that got to do with us tonight? These were Israelites." Yes, but if you're a Christian, you've got a new name. You are a Christ-ian. I wish we had never started pronouncing it Christianity and Christian. That takes the emphasis away. In Christian, *i-a-n* stands for "I am nothing," so we ought to put the emphasis on Christ, where it belongs. We are married to Christ (Rom. 7:4). We've been espoused to one husband (2 Cor. 11:2). When a woman marries a man, she takes a new name. If she's the right kind of woman, she won't want to bring reproach on that name by which she's called. If you're a Christian, you have a new name.

For two spring times I was out in the Ozarks for meetings. What a wonderful place to be in the spring, in those beautiful mountains where Harold Bell Wright used to write some of his interesting books. And the mountain missionary took me about as far back in the mountains as you could go in a Jeep, and he told me about those wonderful mountain people. He told me about old Leonard Lamb, who had been a drunk for seventy-two years, then got saved. It was the talk of the whole neighborhood, even over at the little county seat. They knew about him as he had been, but found it almost impossible to believe that he was a new person. But he was. And Leonard said one day, "I need a little money. Maybe if I'd go over to the bank, maybe they'd let me have a little. They know that I've changed." He went over there, and the banker knew that he'd been converted. They had a talk, and the banker said, "Sign your name on that paper, and we'll let you have a little money." And Leonard Lamb came back home and said, "You know, this is the first time in all my life that my name has ever been worth anything." And you know why? He had a new name. And when Jesus Christ gives you a new name, He changes you from nonentity to identity. You have some importance— not your own, but in Jesus Christ.

In this passage, God says there are four things to do. Four notes make a chord, and I think God wants us to play the whole chord. Some preachers make it appear that to have revival all you have to do is pray. I don't think you can have a revival without prayer, but you can have all kinds of praying and not have revival. I don't minimize prayer. I think it's the thermometer of a church. What a church is on Wednesday night is what it is, not what it is on Sunday morning. You can't tell much about a church on Sunday morning. You've got the morning glories and all the rest of them. But it's Wednesday night when you can find out what a church is like—how many people care enough to come to pray. And it's the measure of a Christian, it's the measure of a preacher. Somebody has said, "What a preacher is in his prayer closet is what he is." That's well said.

I've been in some prayer meetings that were a waste of time. There were at least two like that in the Bible. In Exodus 14:15 Moses stood before the water, and the Egyptians were coming up behind them. Moses was in prayer because God had said, "Wherefore criest thou unto me? Speak to the children of Israel that they go forward." There's a time to pray, and there's a time to proceed. When it's time to proceed, quit praying and start proceeding. Some people never do that, they just pray and that's all. Remember after the battle of Ai, Joshua lay on his face before God. That's a good posture to be in. But God said, "Get up; wherefore liest thou thus upon thy face?" (Josh. 7:10). In other words, there was no time for this kind of a prayer meeting—Israel had sinned. When any church is tolerating sin and won't do anything about it, individually or corporately, the prayer meetings won't do any good, and revival is not going to accomplish anything until we face sin in our individual lives and in the church.

God says here, "If my people shall humble themselves." I don't know of anywhere in the Bible where you're told to pray for humility; you can take care of that. "Humble themselves." Don't sit around and wait for a lovely feeling to come over you and make you be like you ought to be. That'll never happen. There are things that you are to do. Humble yourself as a little child (Matt. 18:4) "under the mighty hand of God" (1 Peter 5:6), "in the sight of the Lord," (James 4:10). Southern Baptists are bad about bragging. We brag an awful lot. I think we ought to have one of our conventions in Los Angeles. They've got a lot of smog out there, and I think we could blow it out in three days. I believe that if we would only humble ourselves, it would spare us humiliation. God's Word does not say justify yourself, it says judge yourself that you be not judged.

The great old evangelist Mel Trotter was saved from the uttermost. As a drunk he had sunk to the lowest stripe of society, but God saved him. Trotter didn't put up with any runaround. He was having a prayer meeting and everybody prayed but one man. Mr. Trotter said, "Pray, brother." The man said, "I can't." Mr. Trotter asked, "What's the matter?" "Nothing," said the man. "I just can't pray." Mel said, "Get down on your knees and confess your sins." The man said, "I just can't think of anything, Mr. Trotter." Mr. Trotter said, "Get down there on your knees and guess at it." The man got down on his knees and guessed at naming his sins and hit it the very first time. You know, if people today would turn off television long enough to give God a chance to speak to their hearts, the first

thing they'd think of, no doubt, would be the sin that's caus-
ing them trouble.

Then this passage says, "If my people shall seek my face."
God says in Hosea 5:15, "I will go and return to my place, till
they acknowledge their offence, and seek my face." And the
psalmist said, "When thou saidst, Seek ye my face; my heart
said unto thee, Thy face, LORD, will I seek" (Ps. 27:8). Seeking
God's face means to seek the smile of God and His approval
so that He makes His face to shine upon us and lifts up the
light of His countenance on us and gives us peace. "Nothing
between my soul and the Savior, so that his blessed face may
be seen." A black preacher in Philadelphia wrote that song.
His son led the singing for me in several meetings in Grand
Rapids and Toledo and Rockford, Illinois, and I love to hear
him sing his daddy's songs, like "Take your burden to the Lord
and leave it there." And this one, in particular, "Nothing between my soul and the Savior." It's a great song. We could have
revival anytime if we didn't have to lose face to have revival.
Nobody wants to lose face.

Revival begins when people, in humility, get right with God
and with each other. That's what it boils down to; there isn't
anything else to get right with. That's where the cross comes
in. The cross has a vertical beam, "Thou shall love the Lord
thy God." It has a horizontal beam, "Thou shall love thy neigh-
bor as thyself." And on these "hang all the law and the prophets" (Matt. 22:37–40). When you get straight on those two
things, you're straight. I'm not a Catholic. I don't carry a cru-
cifix, but many times in my walks (and I walk an awful lot) I
find myself doing a little inventory of my own soul. And I say,
Lord, how am I doing *this* way and how am I doing *this* way?
And that's perfectly proper. Have you tried that? Is there anything in your life between you and God where you're not in

agreement? Is there something in your life that God wants you to do that you won't start doing, or He wants you to quit and you won't quit it? Get right with God.

Is there anything between you and anybody? Jesus said, "If thou bring thy gift to the altar, and there rememberest that thy brother hath aught against thee; Leave there thy gift before the altar, and go thy way; first be reconciled to thy brother, and then come and offer thy gift" (Matt. 5:23–24). That sure would ruin some offerings on Sunday morning over the country. Get right with your brother. It doesn't matter whose fault it is; the Lord didn't go into that. It takes more religion to apologize to somebody than it does to give a hundred dollars to foreign missions. It's difficult just to say, "I was wrong, and I'm sorry, and I want you to forgive me." Husbands and wives ought to go home and start a revival there in the home by saying, "I've not been the husband I ought to be," or "I've not been the wife I ought to be," or "I've not been Christian." Sometimes young people need to go to Dad and Mom, say, "I'm sorry," and ask for forgiveness, and sometimes the parents need to say it to their children. That's when revival begins.

One woman said that she had been the teacher of a Bible class for ten years before she ever got right with God. She said, "I went to an old Methodist altar and knelt and said, 'Lord, I'll go anywhere. I'll go to Africa; I'll go to India. I'll go anywhere.'" God said to her, "I don't want you in Africa. I want you to get right with Susie right here in the church." She hadn't thought about that. She said, "I'd rather have gone to Africa than get right with Susie." The Lord said, "Get right with Susie right here in the church." And they didn't have a revival until she got right with Susie.

During some meetings in Pennsylvania years ago, we had a spiritual dry spell for two or three nights. If I hadn't had a glass of water on the pulpit and if there hadn't been a little humidity in the air, those meetings would have dried up and blown away. I said, "Lord, give us something, anything would be better than nothing. Give us a revival or a riot or something, but give us something." And I gave an invitation, and one of the prominent members of the church walked down the aisle and faced the people and said, "I want to confess some of the ungodly things I've said about our former pastor." I said, "Now, we're going somewhere." The old Adam never walks down the church aisle and says things like that. That's the new person, and that's Jesus, and that's the Holy Spirit speaking through that person.

Our text says, "And turn from their wicked ways." You don't hear much today about wickedness. It's been said that we can't expect God to take away sin by forgiving it if we're not willing to put it away by forsaking it. That's well said. "He that covereth his sins shall not prosper: but whoso confesseth and forsaketh" (Prov. 28:13)—give them up, quit whatever is wrong and start whatever is right, that's the person who shall have mercy and shall prosper. "Well," you say, "what kind of sins?" Every kind. The sin of omission: "For the good that I would I do not" (Rom. 7:19). What is it that you know you ought to do that you've never been willing to do? You could fill the front of the church with sins-of-omission confessors. What is it that you know you ought to do and you won't do it? People don't like to be told what they ought to do in the home or in school or in church. But the Bible doesn't hesitate to tell us what we ought to do. We ought always to pray, to obey God, to forgive, to love one another, to support the weak, and so on. And when God says something like that, it's not a suggestion, it's a commandment. And "to him that knoweth to do good, and doeth it not, to him it is sin" (James 4:17). It's just as wrong *not* to do what you *ought*, as to *do* what you ought *not*.

Now consider the sins of commission—the other side of the coin—the thing that you do that you ought not. Romans 7:19 speaks of the sin of commission when it says, "The evil which I would not, that I do." They tell us that we preachers today should never do any negative preaching, that we should preach only positively. I'd have to throw away a good portion of my New Testament if I left out the negatives. The Bible is double-barreled all the way through. It talks about the righteous man who "walketh not in the counsel of the ungodly, nor standeth in the way of sinners, nor sitteth in the seat of the scornful" (Ps. 1:1). Nehemiah said, "So did not I, because of the fear of God" (Neh. 5:15). Paul said, "Walk not as the Gentiles" (Eph. 4:17). "Be angry, and sin not" (v. 26). "Steal no more" (v. 28). "Let no corrupt communication proceed out of your mouth" (v. 29). "Grieve not the holy Spirit" (v. 30). No filthiness, foolish talking, and jesting (5:4). "No fellowship with the unfruitful works of darkness" (v. 11). "Be not drunk with wine" (v. 18). "Put on the Lord Jesus Christ" (Rom. 13:14)—that is positive, but Paul ends with the negative, "and make not provision for the flesh to fulfill the lust thereof." Sometimes that lust is a very small thing. Somebody put it this way: "The shelf behind the door, the shelf behind the door, tear it down and throw it out; don't use it anymore, for Jesus wants His temple clean from ceiling to the floor. He even wants that little shelf that's hid behind the door." What in your life needs confession? And it's sometimes just one evil.

I was in some meetings at Capitol Hill Baptist Church in Oklahoma City, and a young fellow came down the aisle and took my hand, putting a pack of cigarettes in my pocket. He said, "I realize they don't belong in the life of a Christian. I see that tonight, and I'm giving them up." I hadn't preached on tobacco. Do you think I'd waste a sermon on tobacco? I always tell them if they've got their tobacco with them to leave it out on the steps, and I'll guarantee them no hog or dog will get it before they go back out after the meeting. But I wouldn't waste my time preaching about tobacco. But that old boy was convicted about tobacco because that's where the trouble lay. So whatever it is, deal with it.

The Bible says, take up your cross and follow Jesus (Matt. 16:24). You can come to Jesus and still not be saved. Do you know that? Because He said, "If any man come to me, and hate not his father, and mother, and wife, and children, and brethren, and sisters, yea, and his own life also, he cannot be my disciple" (Luke 14:26). I preach a lot about the other side of the coin. All money has two sides. You never saw a one-sided quarter in your life. And every truth in the Word of God has two faces: the sovereignty of God and the responsibility of man; faith, works; Jesus, son of God, Jesus, son of man. All the way through, it's both sides. And we need to see both sides of this picture.

Sometimes we're afraid of the quote Jesus said: "If any man come after me, let him deny himself and take up his cross and follow me" (Matt. 16:24). If you don't do that, it's pretty evident you're not coming after Him. You may have come to Him, but you're not coming after Him. We don't like the cross. I heard the other day of some youngsters—quite young—who were supposed to put on a program one night at church. They all lined up and they were supposed to come marching down the aisle and then remain standing and sing. They were supposed to march in singing, "Onward, Christian Soldiers." The youngsters took a notion that each one would carry a little cross. But the music director didn't like that idea, so he took away their crosses and set them behind the door to one of the rooms. Well, the kids didn't like that, and one of their leaders got them together to stage a sort of counteraction. When they came marching down the aisle they sang, "Onward, Christian Soldiers marching as to war, with the cross of Jesus hid behind the door." I don't blame them, and sometimes we do hide the cross of Jesus behind the door. And yet we say, "I'm a Christian." Well, what is a Christian?

There are sins of omission, of commission, and of disposition. Second Corinthians 7:1 says, "Having therefore these promises, dearly beloved, let us cleanse ourselves from all filthiness of the flesh and spirit, perfecting holiness in the fear of God." The sins of carnality that Paul mentions are all sins of the disposition and of the spirit: "envyings, wraths, strifes, backbitings, whisperings, swellings, tumults" (2 Cor. 12:20).

Some dear people wrap the rags of their self-righteousness around themselves because they don't do this sin and don't do that sin, but that's all they say. You feel like saying, "Well, what *are* you doing to the glory of God?"

Is your heart right? The Bible tells us we were predestinated to be conformed to the image of God's Son. God saved you to make you like Jesus. How is He coming along? Are you any more like Jesus than you were ten years ago? We're to be like Him. It's not how pious you look at the Lord's Table once a month. It's how you act at the breakfast table. If it takes two cups of coffee to make you fit to live with, you better get in a revival, because those are the things that show up disposition.

Finally, there are the doubtful things: "Whatsoever is not of faith is sin" (Rom. 14:23). You say, "Well, there's something in my life that I don't know about. Sometimes I think it's all right, and then I don't know." In that case, get rid of it, or at least put it in God's hands. If it's all right, He'll give it back to you, and if it's not, you don't need it. But be honest about those habits of life, whatever they are and however harmless they seem. The Lord will take care of them.

When I was a boy, my dad took me to an old water-powered mill. I liked to see the stream-fed channel of water pour over the big waterwheel. The turning waterwheel powered gears that turned the massive millstone to grind the grain. Suppose one day there wasn't enough water to turn the wheel. The millwright would look silly if he jumped on the wheel to try to make it go round. He could go up the creek and deepen the channel. If that was the problem, the water would once again flow over the wheel and he'd be back in business.

I travel all over the country to all kinds of evangelistic conferences with preachers and educators, musicians, and Sunday school superintendents. They are trying to make the wheels go around in the church, and the wheels are not turning much. One trouble is that we fail to remember that all the wonderful things you read about in the Acts of the Apostles were simply the outflow and overflow of the inflow of the Holy Spirit. Jesus said, drink of this living water and from within such a person will flow rivers of living water (see John 7:37–38).

The church these days needs to go up the creek and get sin out of the way in our lives. Then the Spirit will flow. There isn't any other way. So I say to people, "You say you want a revival here in the church. Are you willing to pay the price of revival?" God is not running a fire sale and a bargain counter. A revival costs something. It costs a lot. I'm not wearing myself out to go all over the country preaching a cheap Christianity. Salvation is free, but it's not cheap. Let's get that straight. It cost God the Son His life, and it'll cost you every blessed thing you've got to be a New Testament Christian. We've got a strange doctrine today that I can take Jesus as my Savior and won't go to hell, but I'm not going to be out and out for Jesus. If you're not going all out, you might as well stay out, because Jesus Christ said discipleship is all-out, total, absolute commitment.

A Christian is a brand new somebody. You belong to Jesus Christ, lock, stock, and barrel. You're not your own. You're bought with a price. Not a thing in this world belongs to you. It is not *your* health, *your* mind, *your* money, or *your* job, because when you belong to Jesus, you're His. If we ever get church members to see that ownership, they no longer will be satisfied with an hour on Sunday and reading the Bible once in a while and praying in a jam. People are called to make commitment the regular practice of their lives. Some, thank God, do understand, but it's too few.

I ask you, "Do you want to see a revival?" How much do you want to see a real revival in this place? Are you willing to say, "I want to see a revival in this church. I want it enough that I'm willing to pay my part of the price in humbling myself, and praying, and seeking God's face, and turning from any evil way. I'm willing to turn from what's wrong and start doing what's right. I'm willing to do what God wants me to do. I'm willing to turn my life completely over to God and let Him straighten it out"?

That's the test of revival.

Chapter 3

IT'S ABOUT TIME

$\mathcal{D}$id you ever look for a letter that just wouldn't come, or for a friend who never showed up, or for an appointment that you couldn't get? Then one day it happened: The letter came. The friend showed up. The appointment came through. But by that time your patience was exhausted, and you were in an ugly mood. All you could say was, "Well, it's about time." On that subject, I'd like to use three texts:

> It is time for thee, LORD, to work: for they have made void thy law. (Ps. 119:126)

> Sow to yourselves in righteousness, reap in mercy; break up your fallow ground: for it is time to seek the LORD, till He come and rain righteousness upon you. (Hos. 10:12)

And then the more familiar Romans 13:11b:

> It is high time to awake out of sleep: for now is our salvation nearer than when we believed.

Civilization reminds me of an ape playing with a blowtorch in a room full of dynamite. We're living in a day of guided missiles and misguided men, and in America we have painted ourselves into a corner. I was in meetings in Jacksonville, Florida, when a space mission was launched. I watched the astronauts go into space on the TV in the corner of my room, but I could look out the window into a park where I dared not take a walk. I thought of the paradox of it all. We are smart enough to walk on the moon and not safe enough to walk in the park.

Louis Evans visited a missile defense base in New Mexico. The engineer told him a little—about as much as he thought a preacher could take in—of what it takes to launch one of these monsters into the elements. After he had finished, he turned to the preacher and said, "If you're a man of God, pray for me. My wife is leaving me tomorrow, and our home is breaking up." He had enough expertise or know-how to perform tasks that almost seem miracles, and yet not enough to keep his family together. That's the situation we face today.

We've built a complexity to life that we don't know how to handle. Close to the river in Knoxville, Tennessee, a Hyatt House hotel was built in the Aztec style. It slopes in front, so that it looks like a dam. They say that a drunk staggered up to look at it some time ago and said, "I knew TVA [the Tennessee Valley Authority electricity generating project] would build a dam that missed the river." Well, something like that happened in America. We've never been in a worse fix, generally speaking. The experts have all the answers, but they don't even know what the question is. Our machinery has gotten ahead of our morals, and science doesn't have the answer to sin. And our problem today is what it's always been—sin. Science doesn't have an answer for that. It's about time that we discovered that God has provided an answer, and it's all set forth in these three verses.

I sat up for three hours some time ago watching TV late at

night, and I'll never do it again. Think how many commercials you have to hear in three hours. But it was a film adaptation of William L. Shirer's book, *The Rise and Fall of the Third Reich,* the life of Adolf Hitler. I sat there transfixed, watching thousands upon thousands of Germans in phalanx formations, standing hands up, *"Heil Hitler,"* before that human aberration. The historian Arnold Toynbee said that he couldn't understand how a nation as literate as Germany—the land of Ludwig von Beethoven, the land of Martin Luther—could turn over its boys, its money, and its government, turn over everything to this wild man. He almost ruined the world with the power that was given to him. Toynbee sounded like a Baptist preacher when he concluded, "There must be a vein of original sin in human nature. Civilization is only a thin cake of custom overlying a molten mass of wickedness, always boiling up for an opportunity to burst out."

That's right. That's the explanation of the fix we're in. You won't hear it discussed in the United States Congress. You won't hear it in the United Nations. In fact, you can't even pray out loud in that place. You won't find the answer in the universities. You won't find it in the scientific centers. But it's in this text. Here's the trouble: We have made void the law of God.

The preacher Ben Haden said, "Right will always be right even if nobody does it, and wrong will always be wrong even if everybody does it, because God does not change. The Scripture cannot be broken." God has given to us certain laws—physical, moral, and spiritual. You may not like the way some of them operate, but that's the way it is. "Be not deceived; God is not mocked" (Gal. 6:7).

For instance, marriage is the basis of society. The home is the foundation for our natural life. And yet today an increasing number of men and women live together as husband and wife without even going to the trouble to get married. That's not the way of God, and you can't break the law of God. Nobody ever *broke* the law of God. You *break yourself* against the law of God. You might as well attack Gibraltar with a popgun as to go up against the law of God in your own little weak self. You can't do it. You can't jump over a skyscraper. You don't break the law of gravity. You can break your neck—but break the law of gravity? And there are those today who think they can be immoral and escape the consequences. There are some very clever ways of escaping some of the results, but none for escaping the consequences. And so we reap a harvest of diseased bodies and cooked brains and blasted lives and broken homes and teenager suicide.

And let me say while I mention teenagers, that I've been preaching for a long, long time, and I have a better response today from youth than I've ever had, and that's covering a good deal of years and territory. I think that the average young person today is sick and tired of a lot of this garbage. They've been living through, or in, and sometimes partaking of it all, God help them. But they appreciate authority from someone who is not a phony, who practices what they preach. They didn't create this situation, anyhow. They inherited it. And you know where they got it. So they do need a hero. The eternal Hero, if you want to call Him that, is ready to help them anytime. We all need that Hero. More than ever we need Him so that we can face homosexuality, drug addiction, pornography, and crime that makes the streets unsafe to walk even in daylight.

I grew up in the foothills of the Blue Ridge Mountains, in the old country church neighborhood. When my family went to a meeting of our revival in August, we never locked up the house. Nobody was going to break in. Everything was safe. Now I live in motels, and I was in one in which the security staff had attached the telephone to the table with screws. You hear about that woman who said, "What in this world are we coming to? Somebody broke into my house and stole all of my Holiday Inn towels." There would be no room in the jails to hold all the criminals, if we could catch them. There would be no time to try them. The court dockets are already too loaded. Capital punishment is frowned upon, although God Almighty started it. And today the criminals are walking the streets while good people are behind lock and key, trying to stay safe in their own homes. There is no authority in the home, in the school, or in the church. The principal of a high school said recently to the teachers, "Now don't tell the kids to obey. That's out. Tell them to cooperate, but not to obey." *Cooperate* is not the word my daddy used. If I hadn't *co-operated*, he'd have *operated*.

It's about time for God to work in America to straighten out the iniquities and the inequities of this Sodom and Gomorrah. It's time for God to bring to judgment a generation that's laughed in His face, pronounced Him dead, denied His Word, disowned His Son, and turned His holy day into a holiday. It's time for God to show up these "blind leaders of the blind" (see Matt. 15:14), some of whom are in pulpits. He also needs to show up these bland leaders of the bland who dust off sin with a powder-puff and spread cold cream on the cancers of iniquity. It's time for youth to learn that verse: "Rejoice, O young man, in thy youth; and let thy heart cheer thee in the days of thy youth, and walk in the ways of thine heart, and in the sight of thine eyes: but know thou, that for all these things God will bring thee into judgment" (Eccl. 11:9). You have a date with deity and an appointment with the Almighty. You may not have it in your little book, but it's in His. You've got a date coming up with God.

Then the second text says, "It is time for God to work, it is time to seek the Lord. Break up your fallow ground" (see Hos. 10:12). You know what *fallow ground* is. It's ground that's lain idle and is covered with weeds and briars and brambles, and it's unproductive because it's undisturbed. Churches get like that, too. Sometimes I wonder whether we'll ever have another deep revival in such a shallow generation. Somebody asked a preacher some time ago, "How large is your pastorate?" He said, "Twenty-five miles wide and one inch deep." I can understand that and agree with him heartily.

"Oh," you say, "but God can send a revival anytime." Yes, but a lot depends on the soil, and Jesus told us about four kinds of soil, and they represent the human heart. And you're not going to have a crop if you don't break up the ground. If the dirt could talk, it would say, "What does this farmer mean putting this sharp plow into my breast?" But that's the only way you can get on the way toward having a worthwhile crop. And it's true spiritually. I read in the Old Testament that Moab had settled on his laurels and had "not been emptied from vessel to vessel" (Jer. 48:11). The church needs churning up and emptying from vessel to vessel. That's what revival is. It moves us about from our position in which we've become comfortable. Your medicine bottle may say on it, "Shake well before using," and that's what God has to do with His people. Time and time again, He has to shake them up before He can use them. When you put sugar in the lemonade and it's still sour, you know what the trouble is—the sugar is all at the bottom. Paul wrote to Timothy: Stir up the gift of God that is within you (2 Tim. 1:6). Soil is unproductive because it is undisturbed.

I was in meetings at the First Baptist Church of Jackson, Mississippi, some time ago. Dr. Hudgins was pastor then, and as we watched the people go out, he turned to me and said, "Well, we had some subsoil in here this morning." I liked that; got under the crust. That we seriously need. I was pastor for five years to the oldest Southern Baptist church in the South, the old First Church of Charleston, South Carolina. They're getting ready to commemorate their three hundredth anniversary. I used to have chapel over at the Citadel, the military college when General Summerall was the commandant. He was a veteran of World War I and fought alongside Douglas MacArthur in World War II. He was a general out of the old school. He didn't have much to say, but what he said was pretty important. One time we marched out as we were supposed to do, and then the cadets followed. When we reached the door, he took my hand and said, "Thank you. You get under these boys' hides." That's all he said. And I thought that was one of the greatest compliments I ever received, and I've asked God to help me get under the hides and break up the fallow ground and be an instrument in His hands.

Jesus, after all, wants to disturb us. "Behold, I stand at the door, and knock" (Rev. 3:20). Have you ever settled down some evening in your robe and slippers in the easy chair for a quiet evening, and then came the knock, and away went your quiet evening? Our Lord wants to wake up the church today, and the church will do everything on earth but the last thing that Jesus asked the church to do. In the book of Revelation, Jesus ordered five out of the seven churches to *repent*. Nobody wants to repent. The average church puts on a drive for more church members, and they call it a "revival." We've already got too many members of the kind most of them are. We are not going to have real revival until the church repents.

I sometimes want to give up trying to get Southern Baptists to see the difference between *revival* and *evangelism*. Evangelism is the preaching of the gospel to win the lost. I'm not an evangelist. I preach to the church most of the time because that's where it begins, if it ever begins. Revival is a work of the Spirit of God among God's own people, whereby they get right with God and with each other. But we don't want the fallow ground broken up. Revival means conviction of sin, confession of sin, separation from the world, submission to the lordship of Christ, and filling with the Holy Spirit. And it usually starts with the leaders. I used to think revival had to start with the backsliders, in the Christmas and Easter folks. But I found out that it starts with the best people in the church.

Maybe you've heard Bertha Smith tell about the Shantung revival. Dr. Culpepper was a great missionary and a saintly man, but by the time God got through with him in that revival, you'd have thought he was the worst sinner in China, because it starts with those who are leaders. But it's about time today to quit playing church—these meetings that start at 11 sharp and end at 12 dull. Dr. Donald Gray Barnhouse in his book on Revelation points out that Jesus said to that church at Laodicea, "I'd rather you be cold than warm" (see Rev. 3:15–16). That's what Jesus said. He would rather the church be cold than warm today. He said, "I'd rather you be cold or boiling." That's the extreme. They were at about the halfway mark. It made Him sick. He said, "I am about to spew you out of my mouth." That's not elegant, but you get the idea. Barnhouse went on to say that if you're cold, you may get cold enough to hunt a fire, but if you're lukewarm, you're comfortable. You never have a revival in a comfortable church—never. Something has to happen to stir up the saints. Sometimes in the restaurant the waitress says, "May I warm up your coffee?"

and I've got a half a cup that's already tepid, and I say, "No, pour this out and let's start over. I don't want any Laodicean coffee." I don't think she knew what that was, but you do. God doesn't want it either.

It is time to wake up, says Romans 13:11. It's about time for God to work in retribution, because as a nation we've made void His law. And then, of course, He's going to break through one of these days. We face either the return of the Lord or revival or retribution—ruin. Paul Harvey said, "Christians believe Jesus Christ will return and take over when mortals have made a hopeless mess of self-government." Harvey adds that the Lord ought to be back anytime, because we've done it. We've prepared the way.

I'm in favor of any effort to have a little peace, of course. President Anwar Sadat of Egypt did a brave thing when he went over to Jerusalem to speak to the Knesset. I remember when Woodrow Wilson went to Paris to launch a League of Nations. Franklin D. Roosevelt went to the Yalta Conference in February 1945 on the liner *Manhattan,* and some newspaper writer said, "The Messiah is not on the *Manhattan.*" Harry S. Truman went to Potsdam and Lyndon B. Johnson went to Glassborough, Scotland, in 1967, and Richard Nixon went to China in February 1972, and Jimmy Carter went abroad in the cause of peace. I'm in favor of any effort that brings even a little peace, but we're not going to have world peace until Jesus Christ comes back to set up His kingdom here. He must take over this mess that we've made out of creation. Billy Graham says as an American he's a pessimist, but as a Christian he's an optimist. I agree with that. Whoever got the idea that judgment can't happen here?

I'll never forget looking up at the Parthenon in Athens at night in the glow of all the lights that are turned on it. I turned to my wife and said, "Honey, remember that old thing was standing before Jesus came." But what is it now? It's the monument to a civilization that came and went. Greece produced high standards in oratory, art, literature, and other learning. Similar landmarks have been left throughout history. Pharaohs left the pyramids. The Roman Empire left the Colosseum. We also will be a civilization that came and went if we do not settle our problems with the right source. My old daddy had a saying: "Nothing is ever settled 'til it's settled right." Nothing is ever settled right until it's settled with God. That's why our homes are pulling apart. Folks go to psychiatrists and counselors, but they get stuck again with the Word of God. The Word has been ticking for centuries. It sometimes seems slow, but it's never been late. It's set by God Almighty. Heaven and earth may pass away, but it won't. And, thank the Lord, it's on standard time. It's got an alarm of its own, too, and woe unto the poor fool who disregards that warning.

The Bible is a strange old book. Dr. John Phillips says that if you dig into it, you'll have the feeling of an electrician rewiring an old house where the power hasn't been cut off. You'll get a shock, and you'll get a charge if you go deep into this old book: "Now is the accepted time; behold, now is the day of salvation" (2 Cor. 6:2).

We used to sing it in the old revivals:

> Tomorrow's sun may never rise
> To bless thy long deluded sight;
> This is the time, O then be wise.
> Be saved O tonight.
>
> —Elizabeth H. Reed,
> "O Why Not Tonight?" 1842

And Jesus told us about the successful farmer who said, "I'm going to tear down these old barns, build better, and say to my soul, take it easy, thou hast goods laid up for many years." And then God said, "You've got the wrong clock. You're going tonight. You haven't got anything laid up for many years" (see Luke 12:16–20). There's a lot of difference between many years and tonight.

My father spoke to a young man out on the farm about his soul. The fellow said, "Well, Mr. Havner, I'm a young fellow. I've got a lot of time to think that over." Dad didn't believe in fooling around with the things of God, so he said, "You remind me of a fellow in the Bible that God called a fool." That's not exactly the way to do personal evangelizing. You won't find that in any of the books on how to approach sinners tactfully. But two weeks later that fellow walked down an aisle and joined the church. They said, "What brings you here?" He said, "It's what Mr. Havner said. He said I reminded him of a man the Bible called a fool." He couldn't get away from it, and it led to his conversion.

It's worth any price to get a man saved. Don't ever tell your soul to take it easy. That's the worst mistake this farmer made. "Take thine ease," he said. The trouble is that our souls are taking it easy now. We ought to dig up some of these old hymns.

> My soul, be on thy guard;
> Ten thousand foes arise;
> The hosts of sin are pressing hard
> To draw thee from the skies.
> —George Heath,
> "My Soul, Be on Thy Guard," 1781

And that other one,

> Awake, my soul, stretch ev'ry nerve,
> And press with vigor on;
> A heavenly race demands thy zeal,
> And an immortal crown.
>
> —Philip Doddridge,
> "Awake, My Soul," 1755

What time is it? It's time for God to work. It's time to seek the Lord. It's time to wake up.

If this is like churches everywhere else, we have here this morning the morning glories that bloom on Sunday morning and fold up for the rest of the week. I'm probably seeing you for the last time. I don't know who you are, but you might as well wave good-bye. But I hope you will come under conviction and decide to come back and try it one more time, because I'm not here to pass the time away. I haven't got much time left, I suppose, and I could take it easy when I get old. I think I will then. But I can't take it easy in a time like this. Any preacher or any Christian who can take it easy in a time like this needs a revival. When you consider the state of the world, the state of the land, and even the state of the church, it is high time to wake out of sleep.

Chapter 4

SHOWDOWN ON
MOUNT CARMEL

*F*irst Kings 18:30–39 records the dramatic experience when Elijah prayed down fire from heaven, so I begin with the thirtieth verse:

And Elijah said unto all the people, Come near unto me. And all the people came near unto him. And he repaired the altar of the LORD that was broken down. And Elijah took twelve stones, according to the number of the tribes of the sons of Jacob, unto whom the word of the LORD came, saying, Israel shall be thy name: And with the stones he built an altar in the name of the LORD: and he made a trench about the altar, as great as would contain two measures of seed. And he put the wood in order, and cut the bullock in pieces, and laid him on the wood, and said, Fill four barrels with water, and pour it on the burnt sacrifice, and on the wood. And he said, Do it the second time. And they did it the second time. And he said, Do it the third time. And they did it the third time. And the water ran round about the altar; and he filled the trench also with water. And it came to pass at the time of the offering of the evening sacrifice, that Elijah the prophet came near, and said, LORD God of Abraham, Isaac, and of Israel, let it be known this day that thou art God in Israel, and that I am thy servant, and that I have done all these things at thy word. Hear me, O LORD, hear me, that this people may know that thou art the LORD God, and that thou hast turned their heart back again. Then the fire of the LORD fell, and consumed the burnt sacrifice, and the wood, and the stones, and the dust, and licked up the water that was in the trench. And when all the people saw it, they fell on their faces: and they said, The LORD, he is the God; the LORD, he is the God.

Elijah on Carmel sets a pattern for revival today. Drought and famine had beset Israel, and it had rained on neither the just nor the unjust. Wickedness was in high places, and Ahab and Jezebel were in authority. Idolatry prevailed, but God had a faithful remnant. He also had a prophet who called for a confrontation—a confrontation with the priests of Baal. He said, "We'll have to have a showdown before we can have any showers." Have you ever thought that one reason we're not having showers of blessing in the church is that we haven't had a showdown yet? What are you going to do about it—serve God or Baal? Evil has to be dealt with first before we can serve God. Then He will send the fire from above and the water, the showers of blessing.

Elijah repaired the broken altar of sacrifice and put the sacrifice on it. But I want you to notice something that I've never heard a sermon about in my life. Before he prayed down fire from heaven, Elijah did something generally overlooked or barely mentioned even in the commentaries. He poured twelve barrels of water all over the sacrifice and drenched the altar before he asked God for a miracle. Why did he go to all the trouble of having twelve barrels of water poured over the sacrifice? He did it to make it plain that there wasn't any trick to it. There wasn't any hidden fire under the altar. He set the stage so that God might be the only performer. He was out to make God conspicuous. And he said, "Hear me, O Lord, hear me, that this people may know that thou art the Lord God" (1 Kings 18:37). Everything was made as difficult as possible in order that God might get the glory. Elijah didn't build a little fire so that God wouldn't have such a hard time sending a big fire down.

There's a terrific lesson here. Instead of helping God out by warming up the altar, he drenched the place. When God does His wonders in this world, He wants no flesh to glory in His presence, "So then they that are in the flesh cannot please God" (Rom. 8:8). Throughout the Scriptures the miracles that happened to people took place when they put themselves in a position of such helpless desperation that only God could do anything. Joshua 6:1–26 tells how the priests marched around Jericho—perfectly ridiculous—expecting the walls to flatten out. Whoever heard of taking a walled city by such tactics? They even shouted before the walls fell. Anybody can shout after they fall, but they were so sure, they celebrated in advance. Then in Judges 7:1–22, Gideon, with his thirty-two thousand decimated down to a pitiful three hundred with lamps and pitchers, fought. What sort of strategy is that? Today, I suppose the experts would want to raise fifty thousand by a well-organized promotion campaign, and they'd want to make a survey of the Midianites and work out all the logistics before they tried it. David refused the conventional armor of Saul to tackle the Philistine giant and went out with sling and stone (1 Sam. 17:4–51). What sort of business is that? But if Gideon had won by the usual means, they would have claimed the credit, as the Bible says. And if David had gone up against Goliath in his own strength, he would have had something to brag about. But Gideon and David did it so that all the earth might know that there was a God in Israel, not that there was a David in the camp. David and Gideon made God conspicuous.

The conditions today are just about much the same as they were in the times of Elijah. We're living in a spiritual drought. There's a famine of the hearing of the Word of the Lord. Ahab and Jezebel sit in high places. Idolatry abounds. And yet God has His faithful remnant. We need an Elijah who can face Ahab and call a convocation on Carmel, a confrontation with Baal, and a showdown with the forces of evil.

We're a little short on prophets. We need to rebuild the broken altar and put the sacrifice of a dedicated life thereupon. But before we can expect any fire from heaven, we must drench the altar. I've heard plenty of preaching about rebuilding the altar. I've heard sermons about presenting our body as a living sacrifice. But the hardest lesson for anybody in Christian service to learn is that we cannot help God out in the slightest by warming up the altar in the energy of the flesh.

We try to start a fire of our own and think that'll help out God's fire. It won't do it. We're ashamed to be laughed at by the world. We don't dare face the Midianites with Gideon's band, so we *mob-o-lize*. We don't mobilize, we mob-o-lize a multitude who know little and care less about spiritual warfare, who never have understood that the Bible is the Lord's and the weapons of our warfare are not carnal. We're afraid to face old Goliath today with sling and stone. We want to wear the latest equipment, and Saul's armory is working overtime. We must be up-to-date and borrow all the techniques of the world to do the work of God. But you can't organize revivals as you do secular things, as the world puts on its drives and campaigns.

You can't run a church as you would a business corporation. You can't work up mere human enthusiasm to put over the work of the Lord. We all give lip service, of course, to the Holy Spirit: "Not by might nor power, but by my Spirit" (Zech. 4:6). We sing, "Kindle a flame of sacred love in these cold hearts of ours" (Isaac Watts, "Come Holy Spirit, Heavenly Dove," 1707). But actually we're so wired up to our own devices that if the fire doesn't fall from heaven, we can turn on a switch and produce some false fire of our own. And if there's no sound of a mighty rushing wind, we've got the bellows all set to blow hot air instead.

But God answers by fire, not by feelings, not by fame, not by finances. You can blow up quite a blaze today on Carmel. We can do it, yes. But people are not crying out today, "The LORD, he is the God" (1 Kings 18:39).

The world is not stunned at the power of the church today. They're making fun of us. You can build a great church without the Holy Spirit, put up big buildings, raise a lot of money, and take in a lot of members. But we must learn, beloved, that they who are in the flesh cannot please God no matter how cultured or religious or sincere.

Sometimes a lawyer is chosen to teach the Bible class because he's a good talker. But that never qualified anybody for teaching a Bible class. And a banker is selected to be church treasurer because he handles money all week. That's all right as far as that goes, but that's not enough of a qualification. A degree from a music conservatory does not necessarily qualify a woman to sing the solo in the choir. If she's not in the power of the Spirit, she can't sing to the glory of God.

I belong to a church with thirty-eight hundred members

and three-million-dollar buildings, and we've had only two pastors in fifty-eight years. Dr. Clyde Turner was there thirty-eight years and returned on his ninety-first birthday to preach. He wrote a book on the history of the church in which he said that less than a hundred years ago the members were laughed at and the pastor was hissed when he walked down the street. Some time ago, while holding a meeting in that auditorium, I quoted what Dr. Turner had said, and I said, "Now, how come they aren't laughing at us now when we go down the street? The world is getting better? You don't believe that. No intelligent person believes that. Well, then, how come? Because we've developed a low-grade Christianity today that does not bring on the ridicule of the world at all."

We're not confronting old Baal; we're having a summit meeting. We're engaged in dialogue. We're working out a peaceful coexistence. We're not having desperate prayer meetings. Why bother God today? We can do it. And this multitude at Carmel was impressed because it was utterly unthinkable that fire could consume an altar that was soaked with twelve barrels of water.

We're afraid to shock the world today with a miraculous Christianity. We've developed a brand of religion as much like the world as possible so the worldlings won't feel embarrassed when they join the church; there isn't enough difference to embarrass them. They are almost good enough. They don't need a miracle. They just need to join the church.

A new doctrine is going around, *neo-universalism*, that teaches that everybody is saved. They just don't know it. It's our business to go around and tell everybody. We're just giving out information on that point. We've toned down the contrast between the world and the church so that nobody will feel any radical change switching over from Baal to Jehovah.

But there's no miracle about this, and this pagan world today is not standing there looking at us and saying, "The Lord, he is the God." As long as we try to help God perform His miracles, nothing is going to happen.

God doesn't want the altar warmed up. We're calling in all kinds of contraptions from the world and all kinds of entertainment from the world and all kinds of devices to warm up the altar, to get the thing in a good way. Then, of course, we want God to come down. Why, yes, we want the fire from heaven. But let's warm it up. Elijah said douse the thing. Twelve barrels of water, that's almost too much water. Douse the thing. We're decorating the altar today; we're not drenching it. Job abhorred himself and repented in dust and ashes (Job 42:6); Isaiah said, "Woe is me" (Isa. 6:5); Daniel said, "My comeliness was turned in me into corruption" (Dan. 10:8); Paul said, "For we preach not ourselves, but Christ Jesus the Lord; and ourselves your servants for Jesus' sake" (2 Cor. 4:5). Don't forget that the wisdom of God is foolishness to men (see 1 Cor. 1:18–25), and His ways are not our ways and His thoughts not our thoughts (see Isa. 55:8).

An old saint said years ago with unanswerable logic, "If the preaching of the cross is foolishness to the world, that automatically makes the preachers of the cross fools to the world." That's a terrific statement. If you're preaching foolishness, you're a fool for preaching it.

The world can't understand the way God works, any more than the inhabitants of Jericho could understand the strategy of Joshua, or the Midianites the strategy of Gideon, or the Philistines the strategy of David. We try to operate the church like the world in order to be accepted by this age.

Elijah made it perfectly clear with twelve barrels of water that if God didn't come down, Elijah would look like the biggest fool in all history, standing there before all that multitude, expecting fire to fall. If it didn't, you see where that would leave Elijah. But we're afraid to do that today. We say, "Suppose it doesn't fall?" So we'd better warm up the thing. Let's call in the world to sort of boost it up and draw out a crowd.

I believe with all my soul that when we quit depending on our gadgets and gimmicks and stand on nothing but the promises of God, risking our reputation and future on it, staking everything on a miracle instead of on men and machinery and mere money, the fire will fall. We're not here to demonstrate what we can do for God, because the eyes of the Lord run to and fro to show Him strong in our behalf, not to show how strong we are in His behalf. That's an entirely different thing. Buildings and scholarships and statistics and prestige have their place, but they're not of God alone. How many people walk out of church saying, "God is here"? God is way off today.

An old preacher, Bud Robinson, went to a place one time to hold a meeting. It was a dry, miserable week. He was staying with the preacher, and one afternoon the preacher heard him praying loudly. You could have heard him all over the county. The preacher said, "Uncle Bud, God is not deaf." Bud said, "I know He's not deaf, but He's a long ways from this place." We must humbly recognize, as did the old preacher, that unless God draws near and intervenes, all we do is waste time. We may try to interest people in the things of God with committees and promotions and devices and advertising, and pack-the-pew campaigns, and contests and banner bunches, and slogans, and hootenannies, and pin the tail on the donkey. None of it is any good unless the fire comes down from heaven.

We need to appoint one more committee. I'm sorry to have to recommend it. We are overloaded with committees, but we need a water pouring committee to pour twelve barrels of water over all of our devices to discourage all that we're doing. A drenched altar is a pretty soggy-looking sight. If you don't remember anything else that I say, take this thought home with you. It is the drenched altar that God sets on fire. The drenched altar can apply to your own heart, it can apply to your church. I'm not discouraging what we're doing. Whoever did more than did Elijah? I'm not preaching a "do nothing" religion. Whoever worked harder at it than Elijah? But he realized that only God could save the situation. He soaked the altar to make it perfectly plain that any fire that fell would have to come from heaven. Any human effort to make that altar sizzle before God struck it would be a stench in the nostrils of the Almighty. God was able to make it burn, and God resents our trying to make it burn.

I read that the evil but flamboyant Lorenzo II de Medici (1449–1492) of Florence put on a big pageant depicting the coming of the Spirit on Pentecost. They built the stage so that fire would actually fall on cue. He had the twelve apostles all lined up. The play went along fairly well, until the fire fell and set the apostles and stage set on fire. They almost burned the place. They had the wrong kind of fire. Well, we're trying to stage Pentecost today, but a lot of it is playacting, and the multitude is not saying, "The Lord, he is the God."

Carmel was not a performance. It was an experience. One commentator says, "Christianity started as an experience, but it has become a performance." The disciples in the Upper Room didn't spend their time whooping up enthusiasm and working up plans and techniques. They didn't put on a kick-off supper just before Pentecost. They were at the end of the rope. They had been behind closed doors for fear. Unless God intervened, the cause was lost. And, today, we kindle strange fire on the altar (see Lev. 10:1–2).

I see song leaders over America trying to pull a song out of people's hearts when it isn't in there. We can rekindle the fire if we've ever had it. Paul told Timothy to "stir up the gift of God that is within you" (see 2 Tim. 1:6), but you can't start that fire. It's not worked up from down here. It comes from above. We must die to all the efforts of the flesh to please God, and then there will be plenty of use for sanctified enthusiasm, hard work, plans, programs, but only after the altar has been set on fire.

Fruit growers use baskets, and in the church we have to have organization methods and programs. They're important and necessary. But if the fruit crop fails and there's no life in the trees, you're not going to improve matters by buying better baskets. Today we're turning out the best baskets we've ever had, but there's a failure in the fruit crop. And maybe it needs plowing and maybe it needs cultivation and a lot of things. Instead, we're saying we've got the best baskets we ever had. Don't you see how perfectly ridiculous that sort of thinking is?

Some years ago I preached at a meeting of the Sunday School Board [SSB; now LifeWay Christian Resources of the Southern Baptist Convention] in Nashville, Tennessee. The SSB does a tremendous work, getting the literature out to all the Southern Baptists. I preached just like it was an old-fashioned revival out in the country somewhere, because everybody needs the same thing. Dr. Sullivan, who was president of the SSB at that time, began the meeting with a statement I haven't forgotten. He said, "Ball games are not won by plays; they are won by players." You have to have plays and a strategy. But you've never won a ball game by just designing plays; it takes players. I guess our denominations have some of the best plays today that have ever been devised. But the players, the quality of the people who are implementing and carrying out all this paraphernalia, the preachers and Sunday school teachers, still must have a real fire and not an artificial fire. "Behold, all ye that kindle a fire, and compass yourselves about with sparks. Walk in the light of the fire and the sparks ye have kindled. This shall ye have of mine hand, ye shall lie down in sorrow" (Isa. 50:11).

Nowadays, it's assumed that a preacher who has sufficient ability, education, personality, and public relations ability has got it made. Rarely does a pulpit committee ask, "Is the fire of God on him?" I believe in getting all the education you can, developing all the personality you can, learning all the methods you can, then pouring twelve barrels of water over the whole business, because it's only the drenched altar that God sets on fire.

The philosophy of Christianity runs counter to all the wisdom of this world, and whenever anybody tries to use the wisdom of this world to advance the cause of Christianity, he gets in trouble. God's work has to be done by God's people in God's way. And we're a little embarrassed today to just be New Testament Christians. It's kind of out-of-date, and we're afraid that if we get out there and simply expect God to send the fire down, maybe He won't. Then we'll be left there holding the bag with all the world looking on. We're a little embarrassed, so we say, "We'd better prop it up a little; we'd better warm up the altar, and then it won't be so hard for God to send the fire down." But that doesn't present God with any problem whatever. And now if you're inclined, you go back to your churches and do whatever you do back there. But please carry this truth with you—it's the drenched altar that God sets on fire.

Prayer:
Lord, sometimes we get nervous and think that we have got to warm up the altar ourselves. Lord, teach us that nothing is too hard for Thee. And when we have built the altar and laid the sacrifice thereupon, Lord, help us to do the third thing; help us to drench the altar and then say, Lord, now if anything is going to happen you'll have to do it. In Christ's name, Amen.

Chapter 5

WHEN GOD GETS FED UP

*Y*ears ago I heard Billy Graham speak to the preachers of Philadelphia about the first chapter of Isaiah. I've forgotten the message, but I haven't forgotten the timeliness and the timelessness of this great prophet. Isaiah is as contemporary in application as a morning newspaper. The prophet's writing speaks to his own contemporary Judah, but also to any nation, particularly America. Isaiah speaks to the church; to the Christian; and to the unsaved. The prophet begins by describing his own generation as a nation of rebels:

> Hear, O heavens, and give ear, O earth: for the Lord hath spoken. I have nourished and brought up children, and they have rebelled against me. The ox knoweth his owner, and the ass his master's crib: but Israel doth not know, my people doth not consider. Ah sinful nation, a people laden with iniquity, a seed of evildoers, children that are corrupters: they have forsaken the Lord, they have provoked the Holy One of Israel unto anger, they are gone away backward. (Isa. 1:2–4)

A nation of rebels—is there any expression that better describes this generation?

Charles G. Finney used to say that he never cared for the

expression "poor sinners." He said, "A sinner is a rebel against God; he is suffering from heart trouble. The heart is a rebel, deceitful, and desperately wicked. And the carnal mind is enmity against God, not subject to the law of God, neither indeed can be." We've grown sentimental about sin today, but Finney's is the only adequate description of any rebellious nation. And God says, "My people doth not consider" (Isa. 1:3). They don't think. We're living in an unthinking generation. The word *amused* might carry with it the meaning of "not thinking," the negative of thinking. Film and television keep us from thinking. It's the entertainment industry's business, and entertainers have achieved remarkable success. They've kept us from thinking about things worth thinking about.

Isaiah 1:5–6 speaks of moral and spiritual corruption: "Why should ye be stricken any more? ye will revolt more and more: the whole head is sick, and the whole heart faint. From the sole of the foot even unto the head there is no soundness in it; but wounds, and bruises, and putrifying sores: they have not been closed, neither bound up, neither mollified with ointment." Civilization today is from head to foot rotten. That's just about the size of it, according to the Word of God. You remember how our Lord pictured the last stage of history before He returns. It is a decaying carcass awaiting the vultures. That may be a little hard on the evolutionists, but that's what the Word of God says: "There is a generation that are pure in their own eyes, and yet is not washed from their filthiness" (Prov. 30:12).

If we had only that catalog of iniquity in the first chapter of Romans, some optimists might be inclined to say, "That was written some time ago, and maybe we've made some improvement since then." But 2 Timothy 3 describes the crowd that's to be here in the last days, and it's the same old crowd as in Romans 1. We haven't made any improvement whatsoever. It's a revolting picture. Given what most people do in literature and the movies and television, it's amazing what tender sensibility some churchgoers have if the preacher dares to boldly proclaim the Word of God about this sinful generation.

Isaiah deals in irony with the false religiosity of the time: "Hear the word of the LORD, *ye rulers of Sodom*" (Isa. 1:10a). What a thing to call these people. "Give ear unto the law of our God, *ye people of Gomorrah*. To what purpose is the multitude of your sacrifices unto me? saith the LORD" (vv. 10b–11a). Here's a fed-up God:

> I am full of the burnt offerings of rams, and the fat of fed beasts; and I delight not in the blood of bullocks, or of lambs, or of he goats. When ye come to appear before me, who hath required this at your hand, to tread my courts? Bring no more vain oblations; incense is an abomination unto me; the new moons and sabbaths, the calling of assemblies, I cannot away with; it is iniquity, even the solemn meeting. Your new moons and your appointed feasts my soul hateth: they are a trouble unto me; I am weary to bear them. And when ye spread forth your hands, I will hide mine eyes from you: yea, when ye make many prayers, I will not hear: your hands are full of blood. (vv. 11b–15)

You'll notice that God is fed up even with the solemn meeting, and the Israelites thought a lot of that solemn meeting; but it didn't mean anything to God, not in its present condition.

New Testament scholar Dr. John Phillips says that Christianity began as an experience and has become a performance.

And there never has been more superficial interest in religion than there is today, and there has never been less genuine interest. Amos was another preacher who could bring all the power of satire and irony and all the kindred gifts to bear against false religion: "For thus saith the LORD unto the house of Israel, Seek ye me, and ye shall live: But seek not Beth-el, nor enter into Gilgal, and pass not to Beer-sheba: for Gilgal shall surely go into captivity, and Beth-el shall come to nought" (Amos 5:4–5). God is fed up with formalism.

We need an Amos. I read articles that lament our spiritual condition and say, "How we need an Amos." We do, but try preaching like Amos on Sunday morning and see what happens when this generation cannot endure sound doctrine. This generation comes all the way from heartburn to ear itch when we use the Word of God. When our Lord expounded the Scriptures in His day, His hearers had heartburn. But this generation gathers to itself teachers who scratch itching ears. I started out in this ministry preaching from Amos. I spent some barren years in the ministry when God did not bless, and I was not getting it straight. But I learned my lesson, and the Lord brought me back to plain preaching. I had become enamored with some of the modern approaches to preaching, and I came back to my old home in the hills and had nowhere to preach.

My father died that winter and left me there on top of the hill with my mother and the old country store. That's all we had, and somebody robbed it and burned it to the ground one night, and we had nothing. And God said to me, "If you'll go back and preach like you used to and get all these notions out of your head, I'll make a way for you." And I can testify, from that time to this, God has gone before and made a way so that I have never had to take the initiative in soliciting a place to preach anywhere in this land. As I said earlier, I started out preaching with the book of Amos. I don't remember why I landed in the middle of the Bible, beginning with Amos. But that's where the Lord started me. Amos was a country preacher, and so was I. The Lord gave me a refresher course in this great prophet, and among the very first messages I gave is this one. I gave it nearly everywhere.

Homer Rodeheaver once said when we were on the platform together, "You used to preach as though we thought Amos was your best sermon." Maybe it was, I don't know, but that's the pattern the Lord set for me. I know that a pastor couldn't use the exact technique of Amos. After all, Amos was not pastor of the First Church at Bethel. But he did go up there and lay down the law of God in no uncertain terms, and we need that message now. Amos ridicules false religiosity: "Come to Beth-el, and transgress; at Gilgal multiply transgression" (Amos 4:4). He's actually making fun of their religious service. And the prophet says to "bring no more vain oblations." Do you know what a "vain oblation" is? It's your gift to God when you never have given the giver. James Russell Lowell told us, "The gift without the giver is bare." The Word of God says much about givers who have never given themselves to God.

I believe the greatest hindrance to real revival today is Sunday morning Christianity. This kind pays to God the tribute and the tip between 11 and 12 and then says, "Goodbye, God, I'll see you next Sunday." Sunday morning formalism lacks reality. Some time ago I was invited up to Tremont Temple in Boston for a three-day conference. The evangelical pastors who put it on said, "We need somebody to talk about 'playing church'—that awful evil among us." *Playing church*—we've heard the term many times. It's a grievous thing to play church, but that is all that a great many dear people do today.

Hosea, another prophet, said, "Beth-el has become Bethaven." Jacob met God at Bethel. It was the "house of God." Then Jacob came down to Shechem, got into business, and the family got into trouble. God told him to go back up to Bethel. The second time he called it *El Bethel*, which means "the God of the house of God," because God had become more important than a place. That's a wonderful point to reach in Christian experience.

Here Hosea says that the day has come when what was the *house of God* has become the *house of vanity*, the house of idols, the house of nothing. And how often one finds that today. Some churches started out as Bethel and reached such a high point that it was El Bethel. God was more important than the place they met. And then the day came when it was only Bethaven:

> In vain we tune our formal songs,
> In vain we strive to rise.
> Hosannas languish on our tongues,
> And our devotion dies.
>
> —Isaac Watts,
> "Come Holy Spirit, Heavenly Dove," 1707

A false form of godliness is not necessarily formalism. I used to think that verse referred to stiff, starched churches. It could include some of them. But a church may be very informal in its order of worship and yet have the mere form of godliness. There's a front, a facade, with everything in the show window, but nothing is on the shelves.

There are a number of ways in which a church may have a form of godliness without the power. The third commandment, "Thou shalt not take the name of the LORD thy God in vain" (Exod. 20:7), has wider applications than a great many people think. It applies to far more than outright profanity. Plenty of people in church on Sunday morning take the name of God in vain. Do you realize that when we call Him "Lord, Lord," and do not the things He says, we take his name in vain? Worship is vain when we draw nigh Him with our mouths and honor Him with our lips while our hearts are far from Him. We take His name in vain when we sing, "My Jesus, I love thee, I know Thou art mine; for thee, all the follies of sin I resign" (William Featherston, "My Jesus, I Love Thee," 1864) and haven't resigned one single solitary folly of sin and don't ever mean to. When we sing, "Have thine own way, Lord. Hold o'er my being absolute sway" (Adelaide Pollard, "Have Thine Own Way, Lord," 1907), and have never consented to any kind of sway over our lives, that's taking the name of God in vain. There are church members today who don't curse and swear who take God's name in vain on Sunday.

And what shall one say about today's cheap familiarity? On television and elsewhere, God is "the big buddy upstairs." What shall we say of this day when—as some time ago I watched for a moment, because, trying to find something worth looking at, I couldn't bear to look long on such a sight—a whole room of teenagers dancing to "God Bless America." All of this, you see, is a hideous form of taking God's name in vain and scandalizing the cause by such cheapness, by slapping God on the back, as it were, in a cheap and coarse familiarity. A holy and a jealous God despises ritual without reality and expression without experience. Profanity may be more shocking, but this familiarity is subtler. You can't get away with it, though, because God will not hold him guiltless who takes His name in vain.

There's a bright side to this picture. Isaiah 1:9 tells us that

God had a remnant: "Except the LORD of hosts had left unto us a very small remnant, we should have been as Sodom, and we should have been like unto Gomorrah." A lot of our dear friends today in the professing church don't seem to understand that God is in the remnant business. God is not converting the world, never has set out to convert the world. Pentecost was a great experience, but it did not make a Christian city of Jerusalem. Jerusalem went on to judgment. That book-burning revival they had at Ephesus was a great occasion, but Ephesus remained a pagan city, and so did Pergamum and Thyatira and Sardis. Yet, at Sardis there were those faithful few, the remnant of true believers. It has always been that way.

When I start meetings on Sunday morning, the building usually is full of church members. I might as well wave good-bye to some of them until next Sunday morning. The average congregation includes both the faithful and the visitors. If the average church had to depend on two-thirds of its members, it couldn't operate. The "visitors" group includes those who come during the holiday seasons of Christmas and Easter, the holly-and-lilies crowd. But I would also include in that number the Sunday-morning-only crowd. Back of all those are the faithful, who really keep things going—the remnant.

Our God tells His people that they need cleansing: "Wash you, make you clean; put away the evil of your doings from before mine eyes; cease to do evil; learn to do well; seek judgment, relieve the oppressed, judge the fatherless, plead for the widow" (Isa. 1:16–17). Too many church members have been starched and ironed without being washed. The cleansing process was never started right. Then Isaiah goes on to say, "Relieve the widows." Notice that the cleansing process comes in verse 16, followed in verse 17 by "learn to do well; seek judgment, relieve the oppressed, judge the fatherless, plead for the widow." Every once in a while someone says, "I don't have to be a Christian. I don't have to be in the church. I belong to an organization that believes in a god, and we do a lot for widows and for orphans." The devils believe in God and tremble (James 2:19). These poor fellows don't even tremble. If you haven't been to the fountain filled with blood, all your checks to widows and orphans won't save your soul.

Notice the order that's given here. But the climax comes in Isaiah 1:18: "Come now, and let us reason together, saith the LORD: though your sins be as scarlet, they shall be as white as snow; though they be red like crimson, they shall be as wool." God invites us to talk it over: "Come now, and let us reason together." We reason within ourselves plenty. That's what Naaman did when he went to be healed of his leprosy, and Elisha didn't come out and bow and scrape before this captain; he just told him to go dip in the Jordan (2 Kings 5:9–11). Naaman said, "Behold, I thought . . . ," and he almost missed his blessing by reasoning with himself.

Remember the parable character who reasoned within himself, the rich farmer, the rich fool who thought within himself, "What shall I do?" (Luke 12:17). Notice the pronoun; notice how big "self" is in this picture. "*My* barns . . . *my* fruits . . . *my* goods . . . *my* soul. I'll tell *my* soul, 'Take it easy' with goods laid up for many years." And then God said, "Thou fool." Not "many years," but "this night."

This rich farmer thought within himself, and we reason among ourselves. The disciples reasoned because they had no bread, and Jesus challenged them about it (Matt. 16:8). I think Jesus' question to them ought to be hung on the wall of every committee meeting room: "Why reason ye among yourselves?" I can see my Lord looking over most of our gatherings today, these committees and church convocations where we reason but don't get anywhere. I can hear Jesus ask, "Why reason ye among yourselves?" Why should we discuss why no one brought bread in the presence of Him who provides all bread? We also reason among ourselves as to who will be greatest. The disciples reasoned about which of them should be greatest (Luke 22:24–27). Such thinking was an abomination to God, just as Jesus would today condemn all the ecclesiastical politicking and wire pulling and networking to know the right people. Through Isaiah, God says, "Come and let's talk it over," not on the basis of our reason, but on the basis of His revelation.

This doesn't mean that you have any suggestions to offer to almighty God. When you go to the doctor's office, the doctor wants you to talk over your case. He doesn't expect that you will offer a diagnosis and prescribe treatment, however. Some people almost behave like that when they go to see the doctor. But the doctor does want you to talk it over. And I'm so glad that the Great Physician who now is near, the sympathizing Jesus, wants you to come and talk it over with Him. They did talk things over with Jesus when He was here on earth. They brought their sin and their need to Him. "I must tell Jesus," the old song says (Elisha Hoffman, "I Must Tell Jesus," 1893); and you must, and you should, and you may. He wants you to talk it over. Prayer is not a soliloquy. We're talking with the Lord.

A physical checkup and a spiritual checkup follow pretty much the same pattern. The last time I went to the Mayo Clinic, I was reminded of this. We must have a sense of need. We must have confidence in the physician. We must submit to examination. We must accept the diagnosis, and we must take the treatment. That holds for our spiritual needs. That's the way to have a revival. Whenever a church comes to a sense of need and submits to the examination with confidence in the Great Physician, as Jesus gave the churches in Revelation 1–3, and then takes the treatment, that is revival. That's exactly what revival is. It's not a lot of whooping and hollering. It's not singing songs and preaching and many people joining church. It is the church; it is Christians going through God's clinic. It means talking it over with God at His clinic. It means confessing our sins: "He that covereth his sins shall not prosper: but whoso confesseth and forsaketh them shall have mercy" (Prov. 28:13).

Job said, "Surely I would speak to the Almighty, and I desire to reason with God" (Job 13:3). Job had lost out in the lower courts, and he said, "I'll make my appeal to the highest tribunal. I want to talk it over with God." But let me give you the warning found in Isaiah 1:19–20: "If ye be willing and obedient, ye shall eat the good of the land; But if ye refuse and rebel, ye shall be devoured with the sword: for the mouth of the LORD hath spoken it."

Our nation has never been in greater peril. Will God use the anger of another nation to devastate our land before we come to our senses, and would even that bring us to our senses? Christianity began in Palestine. It's a mission field. The territory of the seven churches is now barren and desolate.

You may find more vital Christianity in Korea or under communist persecution or in Africa than in America. Will they have to send missionaries to us? I don't know. We're having a revival of everything except genuine Christianity, and it's time certainly to talk it over with God.

Having invited us to reason with Him, the Lord has the cure, of course, to every one of our ailments, and you're not going to settle your trouble until you meet with God. That's why we're in the mess we're in tonight. There's a vacant chair in all of our deliberations today. We settle at the lower level, so we don't settle. It's not settled right because it's not settled with God. Educational, social, and economic problems, world peace—how ridiculous to imagine that we're going to settle such problems to the clinking of cocktail glasses but with no recognition of the Prince of Peace. All these reforms and projects will come to naught.

How about home problems? We've never had so many. Many homes that are holding together are doing so out of decency and for the sake of the children. There is no love. The thing may have been patched over. The home that prays together stays together. Some families manage to stick together because they don't want word of their failure to get out. The problem is not settled. God's people are beset by a great many home problems. It's amazing how much domestic trouble there is among evangelical Christians. In fundamentalist homes, with all kinds of Bible guides and books on the table, somehow God's Word hasn't managed to get into the daily machinery. The precepts of the Word have not become the practice of the household.

This holds true for crises in the church. Settling with God is the only way church problems will ever be settled. Sometimes problems are patched up in a meeting, because people want to keep the appearance of unity. The problem is patched up, but it is still there. The only way it'll ever be settled is in repentance and in getting right with God and with each other. That, of course, calls for the surrender of pride. That's the last thing a lot of folks want to give up, and so the thing is not settled. It never will be settled until it's settled right, and it won't be settled right until it's settled with God.

Personal problems must be settled the same way. Some fellow says, "I'm going to get hold of myself now and quit my habits and join the church," and he gets only that far. Some people think that's lovely. "Isn't it better for him to do that?" Well, of course, as far as some by-products and some elements of the problem are concerned, it's better for him to straighten up than to keep on in certain habits. But as far as his soul is concerned and as far as the Word of God is concerned, things are never settled and never will be until that man starts right by being born again. Churches take in a lot of people who have straightened up outwardly. They make their resolution and join the church and make a profession of faith and sweep out the house, but seven demons have come back. And the last state of that man is worse than the first.

In a textile factory, signs hung over the machines: "When threads get tangled, send for the foreman." One day a machine did get tangled. The woman who operated it thought, "This isn't too bad. I'm not going to call for the foreman. I think I can straighten this out." But the more she worked, the more tangled it became, until it was hopeless. The foreman came along and saw the situation. He pointed to the sign. "Don't you see that sign right there in front of you?" She said, "Yes, I know it's there, but I thought I could straighten it out. I'm doing the best I can." He said, "Listen, doing the best you can means calling for the foreman." There are people today who are doing the best they can to untangle their home problems and their personal problems and their church problems. The way to do it is to call on the Foreman. "Come now, and let us reason together," says the Lord (Isa. 1:18). That's the only way your problem will ever be settled.

I wonder if some of you today have an unsettled problem in your heart, in your life, or in your home. The problem is sin or habits. There is no victory in your life, nor is the will of God obeyed for your life, your home, your children, your business, or your church. Do you want to settle the unsettled problem? Do you want to settle it right, and do you want to settle it with God?

That's the only way it will be settled.

Chapter 6

AMOS: THE PROPHET WITH A MODERN MESSAGE FOR AMERICA

The prophet Amos was a country preacher, a rustic of the rustics, a herder of sheep and a gatherer of sycamore fruit. He did not belong to the elite nor to the intellectuals, and when he went up to Bethel to preach, neither his clothes nor his sermons were cut according to the popular pattern. He was sensational, but be not alarmed: Sensational preaching is often merely the kind of preaching some preachers don't like because they can't do it.

Out in the solitudes, "far from the madding crowd's ignoble strife," God had laid upon the heart of Amos three burdens. First, under Jeroboam II, Israel had grown rich and, as is usually the case, rotten with the rich growing richer and the poor poorer. Second, over Israel hung Assyria like the sword of Damocles, God's instrument for the chastisement of a rebellious people. Third, there was the burden of a message: "The Lord GOD hath spoken, who can but prophesy?" (Amos 3:8).

Amos preached, because preach he must. As with Jeremiah, there was a burning fire shut up in his bones and he was weary with forbearing and could not stay silent. Pity the preacher who has not the holy compulsion, the heavenly urgency that cries, "Woe is unto me, if I preach not the gospel!" (1 Cor.

9:16c), who, like Peter and John cannot but speak the things that he has seen and heard. Too many, like Ahimaaz, run, having seen only a tumult and so have nothing to say when they speak.

So there came the day when Amos left the backwoods for the boulevards, as it were, and went up to Bethel, the political, social, and religious center of the land. He must have been a picturesque figure, strolling down Main Street, tanned and sunburned and with all the marks of the countryside upon him. But if anybody in Bethel was embarrassed, it was not Amos. Here was no trumpet with an uncertain sound. Here was no preacher of a lavender-and-rose-water gospel, saying, "You must repent as it were, believe in a measure, or be lost to some extent."

He began, "The LORD will roar from Zion, and utter His voice from Jerusalem; and the habitations of the shepherds shall mourn, and the top of Carmel shall wither" (Amos 1:2). He preached a God of wrath and judgment. We live in a sinful generation that does not like to be reproved of sin, that would have us present God as a grandfatherly Being, trotting His children upon His knee and winking at the wickedness of the sons of men. True, God is love, but there is a world of difference between the love of God and an indiscriminate amiability that vainly calls the righteous to repentance. God is not only a compassionate Father; He is also a consuming fire. There is no place in Scripture for a soft and sentimental God. Today the Almighty has been sneered at, hell has become a byword, and the judgment day a myth. But God is still on His throne, the Devil has not resigned, we are punished for our sins as well as by them, and it takes more than the polished exegesis of apostate preachers to remove the wrath of God.

While there is no systematic outline in Amos's prophecy, it

may be stated thus: "The Present Condition," "The Coming Judgment," "The Passing Opportunity," and "The Distant Prospect."

Amos began with the profiteers who sold their righteous for silver, the poor for a pair of shoes (Amos 2:6); who panted after the dust on the head of the poor (2:7); who stored up violence and robbery in their palaces (3:10); who said, "When will the new moon be gone, that we may sell corn? and the sabbath, that we may set forth wheat, making the ephah small, and the shekel great, and falsifying the balances by deceit?" (8:5).

Amos could say everything in America that he said in Bethel and be up-to-date. When a preacher condemns national evils, someone is certain to ask, "What does he know about economic conditions? Let the shoemaker stick to his last." When Paul started on his voyage to Rome, he said there would be a storm; the captain of the ship said there would not be a storm. They listened to the captain and sailed away to shipwreck. Today, men listen to the captain of the ship and not to Paul; to the voice of information, not revelation; to the engineer, not to the evangelist. Belshazzar listens to the soothsayers, not to Daniel. It is the day of the experts who know more and more about less and less; who, if they were all laid in a row, would never reach a conclusion. The professors have failed, but men heed not the prophet.

Next, Amos turned to the idle rich, who then, as do the rich now, lived in palatial ease in a day of misery, lying on beds of ivory, stretching themselves upon couches, eating the lambs out of the flock, the calves out of the midst of the stall (Amos 6:4). They chanted to the sound of the viol (6:5; the margin reads "quaver" for "chant").

The rustic prophet spoke also of those who "drink wine in

bowls, and anoint themselves with the chief ointments" (Amos 6:6). That is again timely in a nation that fills its bowls with legal alcohol and puts the stamp of national approval on that deadly poison that will ruin its children internally, externally, and eternally. As to the ointments, they have long since been the craze in a nation whose womanhood paints gaily without to hide the dreariness within, putting everything in the showcase of the face with nothing in the shelves of the soul. Beauty is a by-product, but America has made it a business. Jezebel is the only Bible woman of whom it is recorded that she painted, and she was a poor example. "Favour is deceitful, and beauty is vain: but a woman that feareth the LORD, she shall be praised" (Prov. 31:30).

Indeed, to the women of the land Amos was no more eloquent in his preaching than usual. Doubtless, he meant them when he said, "Ye kine [cows] of Bashan ... which oppress the poor, which crush the needy, which say to their masters, Bring, and let us drink" (Amos 4:1). What would he say today? Scripture teaches the dependence of woman upon man, but women have become independent. The breakdown of our social fabric is due in no small part to the defection of womanhood. A. C. Dixon used to say that man was the head of the home and woman the heart, but a home with two heads and no heart was a monstrosity.

Amos turned to the home life of Israel and through him God spoke: "I raised up of your sons for prophets, and of your young men for Nazarites. . . . But ye gave the Nazarites wine to drink; and commanded the prophets, saying, Prophesy not" (Amos 2:11–12). Today, family worship has become almost as extinct as the covered wagon. With Dad at the club and Mother at bridge and the youngsters away in the car, someone has said that "the autocrat of the breakfast table is a sovereign without a realm."

There is as much authority in the home as ever, but the children use it. In this day of electricity, a modern home is one in which everything is controlled by a switch except the children. Indeed, God raised up the youth to be His own, but we have given them wine to drink, both literally and figuratively. We have closed the Bible and junked the family altar; duty and discipline are out of date; impulses have supplanted principles; instead of Nazarites we have nihilists!

It is not surprising that such a prophet as Amos should encounter the court preacher Amaziah (Amos 7:10–14). This dignified clergyman objected to such plain preaching, saying to Amos, in effect, "Your rusticity is out of place here in the metropolis; you belong to the backwoods, not to the boulevards. This is the king's chapel and the king's court." Amos replied, "I was no prophet, neither was I a prophet's son; . . . and the LORD took me as I followed the flock, and the LORD said unto me, Go, prophesy unto my people Israel" (vv. 14–15). This is sufficient authority for any man to preach. When Paul was called, he "conferred not with flesh and blood" (Gal. 1:16). We confer with flesh and blood; we seek the approval of men rather than credentials from God. We must choose today whether we shall listen to the Amos or Amaziah type of preacher. Amaziah is still with us in the pulpit, Pollyannas who wear rose-colored glasses, paint the clouds with sunshine, and preach peace when there is no peace. There are many Hananiahs who teach "rebellion against the LORD" (Jer. 28:16b), but few Jeremiahs who will speak only what the Lord says. Of course, Sunday morning benchwarmers cannot endure Amos; they will desert him, sighing, "This is an hard saying; who can hear it?" (John 6:60). Those who cannot stand Amos go down to Memorial Church to hear Dr. Sounding-Brass give book reviews.

It was against such religiousness—form without force and

ritual without righteousness—that Amos cried: "Come to Beth-el, and transgress; at Gilgal multiply transgression. . . . Beth-el shall come to nought" (Amos 4:4–5:5). It is God saying in irony, "For all your formality, your up-risings and down-sittings, it is only Sardis, dead but with a name of being alive, a-jitter with a delirium of statistics, religiosity without reality, faultily faultless, icily regular, splendidly null."

"Woe unto you that desire the day of the LORD! to what end is it for you? the day of the LORD is darkness and not light" (Amos 5:18). So cried the prophet against those who looked for better times around the corner. He pictured them running from a lion to meet a bear, in other words, leaping from the frying pan into the fire.

Today, America faces judgment, and there is no reason to believe that she will fare better than the nations of the past. God declared through Amos, "Destroyed I the Amorite before them, whose height was like the height of the cedars, and he was strong as the oaks; yet I destroyed his fruit from above, and his roots from beneath" (Amos 2:9). God has destroyed the Amorite before us. The wisdom of Egypt, the might of Babylon, the art of Greece, the laws of Rome—these did not save them. America has had her glory, but the god of this age has blinded her eyes. It has been said that Rome's decline began when her citizens left the Forum, where public issues were discussed, and went to the Colosseum, where the prizefights of that day were held. Verily, America has gone to the Colosseum. Having broken the rudder, she heads for the rocks.

In a vision given to Amos, God put a plumb line in the midst of Israel and compared the nation to a basket of summer fruit ripe for judgment. God's plumb line is among us today, and we are not merely ripe; we spoil. All sorts of remedies are being proposed for our national ills, but we treat the symptoms instead of the disease. It is not money that we need, for God's remedy is without money and without price. It is not more education that we need, for the trouble is of the heart, not the head. Politics cannot save us; the average politician's platform is like a streetcar platform—not to stand on but to get in on.

What shall we do? Amos 4:12 gave us the only remedy: "Prepare to meet thy God." In other days, that was a much-used text, but today God is not regarded as a person, and judgment is thought to be a superstition. Men no longer believe they are hastening on to the great accounting, but for all that, we are passing away to the great judgment day. There is a Judge, a judgment, and a standard of righteousness that must be met. But thank God, it has been met in Jesus Christ, who was made sin for us that we might be made the righteousness of God in Him. To receive Him into the heart by simple faith is to prepare to meet God, for clad in His righteousness alone are we faultless to stand before the throne.

Amos was a stern prophet, but his book closes with one of Scripture's brightest passages, as he paints the picture of a restored Israel (Amos 9:11–15). After all, he was an optimist, and there are two kinds of optimism—blind optimism and Bible optimism. Blind optimism looks to evolution and sings, "God's in His heaven, all's right with the world." Bible optimism does not shut its eyes and whistle its way past the graveyard. All is not well with the world, but better times are around the corner—God's corner. We Bible Christians look for a better day, but it is in that Great White City that's soon coming down. The Chicago Century of Progress Exhibition was opened on May 27, 1933, with a ray of light from a representation of the star Arcturus. We are looking for ten centuries of progress to begin in the light of the Bright and Morning Star.

To whom shall we listen, Amaziah or Amos? Men want the

bright side, but the right side is eventually the bright side. Amos was unpopular, but he was right. Today America listens to the voices instead of to the Voice. Instead of inquiring vainly here and there, "Watchman, what of the night?" let us learn in applying this old prophecy to the present condition, the coming judgment, the passing opportunity, and the distant prospect.

Chapter 7

THE DEPARTED GLOW

In the fourth chapter of First Samuel, we have the account of the last sad days of Eli the judge. Eli died, his sons were slain, and the Philistines took the ark. At that time, the daughter-in-law of the judge was delivered of a child.

And about the time of her death the women that stood by her said unto her, Fear not; for thou hast borne a son. But she answered not, neither did she regard it. And she named the child I-chabod, saying, The glory is departed from Israel: because the ark of God was taken, and because of her father-in-law and her husband. And she said, The glory is departed from Israel: for the ark of God is taken. (1 Sam. 4:20–22)

Think with me for a few moments about the departed glow. I'm glad that I spent my boyhood and early years of this century in what have been called the "good years." A book titled *The Good Years* deals with a period just before 1914 when World War I began. We've never been the same since. This country had just emerged from the Spanish-American War as a young and powerful nation. Americanism was personified in Teddy Roosevelt. Life was full of romance before the land became Sodom and Gomorrah from Maine to California. Boys were boys, and girls were girls. You never heard of homosexuals and transsexuals. Marriage was for life, not a temporary arrangement. I still like the sweet old love songs that were set to romance, not to sex. This was before the hideous avalanche of what some call music that splits our eardrums, demonic, both in words and tune. It's not music, just an excuse for not being able to make music. And an excuse, you know, is the skin of a reason stuffed with a lie. We've come a long way since we used to sing "Let Me Call You Sweetheart" (Beth Slater Whitson; Leo Friedman, 1910), "Moonlight and Roses" (Ben Black and Neil Moret, 1925), "I Love You Truly" (Carrie Jacobs Bond, 1901). I like the simple love lyrics. They had their place.

Fanny Crosby was a wonderful hymn writer, but a lot of people don't know that she did not sit around all the time writing hymns. She also wrote popular love lyrics. One can no longer get recordings of music from that era. The novelist Ernest Hemingway said that we are suffering today from writers who can't write, actors who can't act, and singers who can't sing, and they're all making a million dollars a year. That's the tragedy of these times. It's doubtful whether we'll ever return to an age in America when people fell in love with somebody they wanted to live with for the rest of their days, when "sweetheart" was still in common usage, and when lovesickness was a common ailment of teenagers. We may be too far down the road toward the point of no return.

All this gets an extra boost today from what's happened to childhood. *Saturday Evening Post* once published an article, "What Happened to the Magic of Childhood?" (Robina Smith, *Saturday Evening Post*, 9 February 1957). The article's point was that the magic is gone, and it's not the kids' fault. Childlike innocence gave way to precocious kids as role models who made a fortune in TV commercials. I once watched a television program on which a group of kids discussed ecology. They ought to have been out in the backyard playing hopscotch. What a crime to rob them of their childhood. They'll never have it again. It'll never return.

Life itself has lost its ecstasy and degenerated from apathy into agony. During the first half of life you are romantic, and during the second half you are rheumatic. But I've seen folks who are rheumatic become romantic again and lose all their rheumatism. Of course, sometimes the honeymoon gives way in time to the humdrum.

But thank the Lord, I know couples who have weathered the years and are still in love with each other. There are more of them than you might think—wonderful granddads who are wiser than all the books on how to raise children; grandmothers who never thought that they were in bondage when they were keeping house in their younger years. It was the labor of love, in which they found freedom. I find middle-aged people making a go of it today in spite of the world, the flesh, and the Devil. And I find young couples who have made up their minds not to be led like sheep to the slaughter by the pied pipers of perversion.

But I also see the departed glow in churches and in Christian living. Some of the churches today ought to be named "Ichabod Memorial," because that's what they are. They're a memorial to Ichabod. They may have two pulpits and a lot of candles because God's power is cut off. We read that Moses' face shone; Stephen had a face like an angel, and in 2 Corinthians 3:18, "we all, with open face beholding as in a glass the glory of the Lord, are changed into the same image from glory to glory, even as by the Spirit of the Lord." Christian faith has lost radiance. It's a-glare, but it's not aglow. There's brilliance but not radiance.

You remember that Shishak captured Jerusalem when Rehoboam was king, and he stole the golden shields that Solomon had hung there (1 Kings 14:25–26). Gold had hung all over the place. They wouldn't even look at silver; it wasn't thought to be anything in the days of Solomon. When Shishak captured Jerusalem, his eyes fell on those shields of gold, and he made away with them. Rehoboam did not substitute shields of silver for the gold, which would have been a big comedown. Rather he had shields made of brass. Brass shines with a certain radiance, but it's not gold and never will be. And I find a lot of brass as I move from church to church.

Remember the false fire of Nadab and Abihi (Levit. 10:1–2). A certain home had been left vacant. One miserable winter night a poor little kitten crept in. They had one of these imitation fires they had forgotten to turn off, just the bulb in a fireplace, and it looked like fire. The kitten sat in front of it and froze to death. And I've seen people freezing to death in churches before an artificial fire. It's got a certain amount of glare to it.

What causes that kind of condition? How do you get in such a fix as that? Eli was an indulgent father who lost his boys. Mr. Duncan from England's Keswick Convention preached a sermon at Moody Memorial Church on Eli, "The Good Man Who Was Too Busy." A lot of good men are too busy. Eli loved the Lord. He wanted to serve the Lord. He had a conscience, but the boys rebelled. "Now the sons of Eli were sons of Belial; they knew not the LORD" (1 Sam. 2:12). That's a comedown for you, when the sons of Eli became, as it were, the sons of the Devil. They lived in awful immorality. First Samuel 3:1 says, "The word of the LORD was precious." That means there wasn't much of it. It was rare. "There was no open vision." There wasn't much communication from God. When something else sounds from the pulpit besides the Word of God, we're headed for Ichabod.

In this same fourth chapter of 1 Samuel, the Philistines moved in on the Jews. And the Jews said, "We're in desperate straits, let's get the ark" (see 1 Sam. 4:3). So they got the ark, and they thought that would take care of the Philistine problem. But when you don't have the presence of the Lord in the ark, you've just got a box. The Philistines heard the Israelites shouting, "Now we're going to overcome that we've got the ark," and the Philistines said, "Oh, what are we going to do? Their God is there, and he's going to fight against us" (see 1 Sam. 4:5–7). But the Philistines found out that Israel had the box, but they didn't have the Lord. And a church building is just four walls and a roof.

Any church is headed for Ichabod when it relies on "just going through the motions." And when you try to do that, God is not pleased, and nothing is accomplished. Years later, when the ark was being hauled to Jerusalem for King David, the oxen stumbled and Uzzah reached out his hand to steady the ark, and God struck him dead (2 Sam. 6:2–8). Why would that happen? He didn't mean any harm. He just touched the ark. Wasn't it all right for him to steady the ark since the oxen had stumbled? No, something was wrong, because he was the son of Abinadab, and he had lived looking at that ark for twenty years in the house. It had become just a piece of furniture. He was used to it. Matthew Henry says, "Didn't he think he could proudly do as he pleased about it and move it about, because he'd seen it every day for twenty years?" And beloved, there is such a thing as getting used to the things of God. You get so used to them, they don't move you anymore.

In Africa long ago, when diamonds were plentiful, one day a tourist said, "I saw some boys playing with what looked like marbles, and I drew near, and sure enough, they were playing marbles with diamonds." And that's what we do sometimes. We handle the Word of God as though it were something ordinary—playing marbles with diamonds. We go through the motions of the Christian life. We rarely examine the coinage of the Word of God to see whose image and superscription may be thereupon.

The Philistines were temporarily frightened. And the world may be temporarily impressed by Ichabod Memorial churches. But they'll soon catch on, even the Philistines, that the form of godliness is without power. It's not the ark; it's the God of the ark. It's the presence of God that makes the difference. The Israelites shouted. The Philistines said, "We're in trouble. They're shouting; their God must be among them." But what a day of defeat it was for Israel. And I'm asking, are we living in a day of victory today, or are we living in the birthday of Ichabod? What is this departed glow?

The glow is more than theological correctness. That's important. You can't glow right if you don't know right. Jesus said about the Pharisees, "Do as they say, not as they do." Ephesus was orthodox, but they'd left their first love—right but not radiant. You can be such a thing as a fundamentalist—a fundamental, evangelical, premillennial hypocrite. That's a bad kind of hypocrite. This hypocrite knows it all, can't be told anything, and knows what you're going to say before you say it. And unless the love of God is shed abroad there, you'll have a glare, but you won't have a glow.

The glow is more than ethical strictness. I believe in that. And the Lord knows we don't have strong standards of ethics today. The Pharisees had plenty of ethical strictness. They wouldn't even eat an egg that had been laid on the Sabbath. But the Bible says, "Be not conformed to this world" (Rom.

12:2). Having the glow, though, means more than not being conformed to this world. I know some dear people who are not conformed to the world, and they wouldn't do worldly things for anything, but they have not been transformed. And sometimes they're a disgrace to the cause. They're critical and censorious. They've not got a glow; all they've got is a growl.

Consider the Christians who used to spend their money on bridge and now spend it on backbiting. That's not much progress. They gave up cigarettes and took up gossiping. That's not much progress. Too many people who do not love the world the way they *shouldn't* love it, don't love it the way they *should* love it. If you love the world the way God loves it, you won't love it the way you shouldn't love it. "God so loved the world, that he gave his only begotten Son" (John 3:16).

The glow is more than doing religious business. Don't confuse the glow with the sparks that you generate, dashing around in church work from Dan to Beersheba in a beehive of activity. Some people get so busy with report cards and banners and contests and statistics and all kinds of committee meetings. They rush from conventions to church suppers, to choir practice, to rally day, to raising the budget and paying off the debt. They are doing the work of four people in the church because three people won't do any work at all.

Dr. R. G. Lee said that if an automobile had as many parts in it that wouldn't run as a church has people that won't work, you couldn't push the thing downhill. And in the midst of it all, I think about the passage in the Old Testament where a prophet went through a sort of an illustration to reprove Ahab. He said, "I was given a man to keep. I was told to keep him, not let anybody get him, and I got busy here and there, and he got away" (see 1 Kings 20:38–40): "As thy servant was busy here and there, behold, he was gone." And while we're puttering around, beloved, the best things get away from us.

Delinquency and duty—what a lesson we ought to learn from this portion. The failure wasn't because of ignorance. He knew what he was supposed to do.

> A charge to keep I have,
> A God to glorify,
> A never-dying soul to save,
> And fit it for the sky.
>
> Charles Wesley,
> "A Charge to Keep I Have," 1762

Some people don't like that old song. They say we don't save our souls. Well, that's not what the prophet meant in 1 Kings when he pretended to have lost an enemy soldier in order to convict a delinquent king. We do have this business of seeing to it that our soul is saved, and if you don't trust Christ, it won't be, so you have a responsibility. But we know what to do. The failure wasn't because this servant wasn't adequate for the job. He could have done whatever he was supposed to do. The failure wasn't due to laziness; it was exactly because he was too busy, so that his charge got away: "As thy servant was busy here and there" (1 Kings 20:40). Idleness is "the Devil's workshop," they say. So is too much business that is not the Lord's business.

Dr. Jarrett said, "You're not always doing the most business for God when you're busiest." Eli was a good man, but he was too busy. And it wasn't because this man in 1 Kings was doing bad things. They may have been perfectly good things in their time and place, but they weren't important enough.

Some time ago my pastor told about an art student who

was instructed by the teacher, "I want you to go out here on the side of the hill and paint a picture of a sunset." There was an old barn in the landscape, so he started painting that part of the picture. He couldn't get the roof on the barn to suit him. The color just wasn't right. Time went on, and he was still working on the roof of that barn. The teacher came out to see what had become of the student. "What's going on here?" he asked. The student said, "I can't get this barn roof right." The teacher said, "Do you know what time it is? I sent you out here to paint a sunset, not to put a roof on a barn." God has commissioned people to do a real piece of work, and they've been piddling around, painting a roof, ever since.

When are you ever going to snap out of that waste of time and do something significant for almighty God? It's easy to allow the best things to get away. Youth gets away. You young folks shouldn't think that you have been given a piece of life before you're twenty-one to do with as you please. Then you'll settle down. "I'll get serious later on," you say, "but not now. I must have my fling." "Remember thy Creator in the days of thy youth" (Eccl. 12:1). Get an early start at it, because you'll never have it back. It won't return to you. Sometimes our dear ones get away, too, while we're busy here and there.

The same summer that my dear wife went to heaven, I met a worker with my denomination whose wife had died a couple of years earlier. He had traveled all the time, and she stayed at home. He traveled too much, and she stayed at home too much. It nearly killed him when he got to thinking of the hours he could have spent with her if he had been willing to take weeks off or had taken her along with him.

It's a serious thing when all you can do is groan about the touch of a vanished hand and the sound of a voice that is still. Groaning doesn't do much good when you've been so busy that the main thing got away. I thank God that for thirty-three years my wife went with me all over the country. God joined us to work together, to begin with. I don't have that regret, but I can still say "If I had done this, or if I'd only have thought of that." You can drive yourself crazy over that sort of business. But remember that when the best things get away, the opportunity to serve God gets away, too.

A friend in Greensboro was head of the Drama Department of the University of North Carolina. He lived seventy-odd years before he became a Christian. He was a graduate of Harvard, a man well versed in literature. His wife had prayed for forty-five years that he'd be a Christian. And then he got saved in the middle of the night all alone upstairs. It nearly bowled her over when he told her the next morning, "I'm going to church with you, dear." She had prayed for forty-five years for his conversion. He and I became buddies, and we'd go out and eat together. We both liked to write. He became a deacon in the First Baptist Church. He went everywhere bragging on Jesus.

He had a great intellect, and he'd read the Bible all those years. As a teacher of drama, he knew the Bible as literature, but it never had gotten through to his soul. And you know what got me? I asked him whether, during all those years, anybody had ever spoken to him about Jesus Christ? No one had, he said. "You mean nobody ever spoke?" And he said, "Just a praying wife." And I said, "Were you in a revival?" "No." "Did you hear a sermon?" "No, I didn't hear a sermon. God woke me up in the middle of the night and showed me what a lost old sinner I was." God had to visit him. Nobody else would. So the Spirit of God paid him a visit in the middle of the night. Let's not let these precious things get away from us.

The glow we're talking about is not the afterglow of a past experience. Thank God for these mountaintop days we've had.

Paul went to the third heaven, so wondrous He couldn't tell about it when he got back (2 Cor. 12:2–9). If some preachers ever got to the third heaven, you'd never hear the end of it. Some preachers would work up a story about it with illustrations. Paul was up there, and then he dropped all the way to the depths with that thorn in the flesh. After he prayed for relief, God told him, "I won't even answer that prayer, but my grace will be sufficient for you" (see v. 9). Grace is what he needed, after all. Today we need Jeremiah's bone fire and Emmaus's heartburn and John Wesley's heartwarming, but you can't live on yesterday's manna. You must have fresh oil.

"Jesus Christ the same yesterday, and today, and for ever" (Heb. 13:8). George Müller made that middle part of the verse his motto. Jesus Christ is the same today as yesterday and forever. Harry Ironside told about a woman who had something to say in every testimony meeting, and she always began, "Forty years ago. . . ." Dr. Ironside said, "I finally thought I just must go to her sometime and say, 'Lady, hasn't anything happened since? Hasn't the Lord revealed Himself to you since then?'"

You who are scrubbing up the shields of brass, God wants you to have the gold. Moses endured because he saw Him who is invisible. "They looked unto him, and were lightened: and their faces were not ashamed" (Ps. 34:5). The beholding, the brightness, and the boldness—that'll make you bold for the Lord.

What is this glow? Jesus said, "I am the light of the world" (John 8:12). He said, "Ye are the light of the world" (Matt. 5:14). "For God, who commanded light to shine out of darkness, hath shined in our hearts, to give the light of the knowledge of the glory of God in the face of Jesus Christ" (2 Cor. 4:6). "Let your light so shine before men, that they may see your good works, and glorify your Father which is in heaven" (Matt. 5:16).

Shine as lights in this world. The glow is the outshining of the indwelling Christ. When you said to Him, "Jesus, come into my heart and make Yourself at home," that's what the glow is. "Jesus, just be Yourself in me."

"Christ liveth in me" (Gal. 2:20). Now when that happens, let's get one thing straight; you're not an automaton from that time on, you're not a robot. You're you.

D. Martyn Lloyd-Jones was influenced by G. Campbell Morgan. You see Morgan all through Jones's books. Lloyd-Jones said, "You're still you, remember." Paul said in Galatians 2:20, "I live, yet not I, but Christ liveth in me." Christ lives in me; He is my life. But remember that you are not a wooden soldier as a Christian. You still make decisions. You are you, and you have to make decisions. And when you are saved, as Jesus fills more and more of your life, the old Adam is not eradicated, but the new man grows. Whatever you feed and exercise will grow. So let the new man feed on the Word and rest in the Lord and exercise himself to God.

Isn't that the way a child grows? Food, rest, and exercise. You can't grow a child without these three elements. Leave out any one of them and that child won't make it.

That's the way a Christian grows: feeding on the Word, resting in the Lord, exercising unto godliness. Certainly, we must grow. A lot of babies in church today are not in the nursery, and they're a problem. Paul had a problem with them. They're always so fussy, these 150- and 200-pound church babies. When the new preacher comes, they say, "I don't like him. He changed my formula." They can be a lot of trouble. But you can grow and not have the glow. So feed on the Word, rest in the Lord, exercise yourself unto godliness, and then let the light of the Lord shine through you. You don't have to go around with a great big book and say, "I'm a Christian," carrying a Bible big as the Sears and Roebuck Company catalog. You don't have to do that. They'll find it out, or they'll catch on. The word will get around. If He's walking with you and living in you, it'll get around.

What's the secret of the glow? "But we all, with open face beholding as in a glass the glory of the Lord, are changed into the same image from glory to glory, even as by the Spirit of the Lord" (2 Cor. 3:18). The becoming follows the beholding, and the likeness follows the looking. It's all by faith—F-A-I-T-H:

> **For**
> **All** He is,
> **I**
> **Take**
> **Him.**
>
> **For**
> **All** my needs,
> **I**
> **Trust**
> **Him.**
>
> **For**
> **All** His blessings,
> **I**
> **Thank**
> **Him.**

Make yourself a little placard and hang it up where you can see it first thing in the morning.

That glow has departed from so many Christians in churches. As I travel all over the country, I see a lot of activity, things going on, whipped-up enthusiasm, glorified pep rallies, synthetic happiness. Some have the grin, some have the glare, but I don't see Jesus shining through a lot of it. We don't even know that we don't have it. If I tell some of them, "You don't have the glow here," they say, "We don't have what?"

There needs to be a *consciousness* of need, a *confession* of sin, a *cleansing* of the blood, and a *commitment* to Jesus as Lord, then we'll be spirit-filled. And unless and until we are, Ichabod is written over the place. We might as well name the church "Ichabod Memorial."

"Love" is just another way of putting it, love imparted and implanted in our hearts by the Holy Spirit. Love is not everything. You have to deal with the things that are in your life before you get around to the love. Some people say, "Love's everything." No, it isn't. If it had been, why didn't Paul start with the thirteenth chapter of 1 Corinthians? He had to deal with sin in the church before he got around to the love. But you must get around to the love.

I once was pastor of a little country church. Some men who preceded me had gone on to become prominent preachers, but I didn't hear much about them. I kept hearing about Josiah Elliott, so I thought, *He must have been something. I've got to find out about him.* I went back to where my old friend John Brown was farming. John lived back there on the creek, where in 1934 I wrote my first book, *By the Still Waters* (Revell). John was a philosopher. He was the slowest man I ever saw. He had time to talk. Nobody's got time to talk anymore. I would spend an afternoon with John. I ought to have been visiting, and he ought to have been plowing, but we were just talking. Then the next morning I'd go over to where he was plowing, and we just took up where we left off.

I knew John would give me the lowdown about Josiah

Elliott. I began, "John, I don't hear about any preacher here before me but Josiah Elliott. What was he like? What's the secret of his grip on all these people?"

John leaned on the plow handles a little bit, and he said, "He just loved us." He went on plowing, and I made my way back through the old cypress swamp to the highway while the wood thrush was singing his vespers to the end of a perfect day. All I could hear was, "Though I speak with the tongues of men and of angels and have not love, I am sounding brass and clanging cymbal" (see 1 Cor. 13:1). "Good Lord," I prayed, "help me as a young preacher to settle down in the thirteenth chapter of 1 Corinthians." That's a good place to live. And when you live there, you'll have the glow, because it will not have departed. It's the only alternative to Ichabod Memorial.

Father, we thank Thee that Thou dost condescend to come down and dwell in our hearts. We thank Thee, Lord, that we can open the door and say, "Come in and make Yourself at home and be Thyself in me." There may be folks here this morning, Lord, that have lost their glow. They still believe it, they still go through the motions. They may be working harder than they ever were. Lord, Thou knowest what a killing thing church work can be, if it's not in the Lord. So speak to our hearts and show us what's the matter with us and then help us to get rid of the sin and be cleansed with the blood, filled with the spirit, submissive to the Lordship of Jesus, and we'll have the glow. We pray in Jesus' name. Amen.

Chapter 8

THE CHRISTIAN
AND THIS WORLD

*O*ur text comes from John 17, "the high priestly prayer" of our Lord.

I have manifested thy name unto the men which thou gavest me out of the world: thine they were, and thou gavest them me; and they have kept thy word. Now they have known that all things whatsoever thou hast given me are of thee. For I have given unto them the words which thou gavest me; and they have received them, and have known surely that I came out from thee, and they have believed that thou didst send me. I pray for them: I pray not for the world, but for them which thou hast given me; for they are thine. And all mine are thine, and thine are mine; and I am glorified in them. And now I am no more in the world, but these are in the world, and I come to thee. Holy Father, keep through thine own name those whom thou hast given me, that they may be one, as we are. While I was with them in the world, I kept them in thy name: those that thou gavest me I have kept, and none of them is lost, but the son of perdition; that the scripture might be fulfilled. And now come I to thee; and these things I speak in the world, that they might have my joy fulfilled in themselves. I have given them thy word; and the world hath hated them, because they are not of the world, even as I am not of the world. I pray not that thou shouldest take them out of the world, but that thou shouldest keep them from the evil. They are not of the world, even as I am not of the world. Sanctify them through thy truth: thy word is truth. As thou hast sent me into the world, even so have I also sent them into the world. And for their sakes I sanctify myself, that they also might be sanctified through the truth. (vv. 6–19)

We have a new word today. We used to call it worldliness; we now call it secularism—a big word, but it means the same thing. Just as a rose by any other name smells as sweet, so worldliness by any other name is just as bad. There are two extremes on this matter of worldliness. Some people have separated from so many things they've become super separators and can't even get along with themselves. Then there are others who fear the Lord and serve their own gods. I wouldn't think you could do that, if I hadn't read it in the Bible, but you can. You can fear the Lord on Sunday morning from 11 a.m. to noon. You can fear the Lord and then go right out and serve your own god. And it's being done. Many who claim to be the Lord's sheep feel more at home among the Devil's goats. We call them worldly Christians, which is a misnomer to start with. The Bible says, "Whosoever therefore will be a friend of the world is the enemy of God" (James 4:4).

Somebody asked me, "How can a Christian be God's enemy?" Well, I didn't write it, but that's what it says. "A friend of the world is the enemy of God." I'm convinced that a large percentage of those we call worldly Christians are perhaps not Christians to begin with. A sheep may fall into a mud hole, but it is not content to stay there. A Christian may fall into sin but no Christian is satisfied to live in ongoing sinful practice. When you see a person who is satisfied to live in sin, that person's never been saved. The Bible says, "We know that whosoever is born of God sinneth not" (1 John 5:18a). Sinning is not that person's business. A farmer is a person who farms, and a sinner is a person who habitually sins. Sinning is that person's business. This was the case with false teachers who bear bad fruit (Matt. 7:15–20).

We need to get our Bible zoology straightened out. The Bible compares us to a number of animals, and some of the comparisons are not very complimentary. For instance, we are not to be like a mule (Ps. 32:9). The trouble with a mule is the mule is backward about going forward. We have a lot of people like that in the service of the Lord. The sow is at home in a mud hole—not a sheep (see 2 Peter 2:22). After all, the Lord is raising sheep; He's not whitewashing swine. But we're not to judge people. The Lord knows who are His (see 2 Tim. 2:19). Paul goes on to tell Timothy in verse 19, "Let every one that nameth the name of Christ depart from iniquity."

The best evidence that you belong to the Lord is that you hate sin, and you're not satisfied living in it. When a bird looks like a duck, quacks like a duck, has webbed feet like a duck, paddles around in the water like a duck, and keeps the company of ducks, it's hard for me to resist the conclusion that it must be a duck. When a professing Christian would rather be at the movies than at prayer meeting, would rather be reading the trash of this world than the things of God, would rather be listening to offensive and vulgar music than the music of the saints, I'm driven to certain conclusions. You're more or less identified by the company you keep. Where you feel most at home is your native habitat.

The Bible says, "We know that we have passed from death unto life, because we love the brethren" (1 John 3:14). What if you don't love the brethren? Suppose you'd rather be with the other crowd. Well, that's probably where you belong. When Peter and John were let go by the Sanhedrin they immediately rejoined their brothers and sisters (Acts 4:23). Where do you go when you are let go? I'd hate to track down a lot of church members when they get a couple of hundred miles away from home. When Peter got out of jail, he headed for a prayer meeting right away. We gravitate to what lures us most, and eventually we show up where at heart we belong.

Why does the Bible say in one place, "God so loved the world" (John 3:16) and in another, "Love not the world" (1 John 2:15)? Well, the world that God so loved that He gave His son to save is the world of lost souls. And we ought to love lost souls. If people would only love the world the way God loves it, they'd never love it the way they shouldn't love it. But when John says, "Love not the world," we should understand it as this present age, which is under the Devil politically, economically, socially, and religiously. Satan is the god of this age, the prince of the power of the air, the prince of this world. Our Lord came to deliver us from this present evil world. Ephesians 2:2 states that, before we were saved, we "walked according to the course of this world." We're supposed to walk some other direction after that.

Notice four things in John 17. If you had no other help in the New Testament, these concepts would be enough to locate you in this world.

In John 17:6a, our Lord says, "I have manifested thy name unto the men which thou gavest me out of the world." A Christian has been saved out of the world. The Greek word for "church" in the New Testament means the "out-called ones." God is not out to save civilization today. Civilization is not going to be saved. Civilization is a goner. God is calling out a people for His need. We've been saved out of this world system. We've been given a new position with Christ in the heavenlies (Eph. 2:6; Col. 3:3). Our citizenship is in heaven. Jesus said, "My kingdom is not of this world" (John 18:36). When you are justified and adopted, you are taken out of this world and made a citizen of another realm. And your position up there and your condition down here, and your standing up there and your state down here ought to correspond. The Bible says we're pilgrims and strangers, exiles and aliens. Matthew Henry said, "This world is our passage and not our portion." The Bible says that this world is not our rest. "For here have we no continuing city" (Heb. 13:14a). The next time this world offers some of its attractions, just say, "No, thank you, I'm a stranger here." That's a good answer. "I don't belong. I'm just passing through. I'm not a citizen of this world trying to get to heaven. I'm a citizen of heaven making my way through this world."

It makes a lot of difference how you look at it.

The biographer of G. Campbell Morgan [probably Jill Morgan, *A Man of the Word: Life of G. Campbell Morgan,* n.d.] says of the noted expositor's father that he lived with a Bible in his hand and his face toward a better world. That's a good way to live. Some time ago I got into an old-fashioned Methodist camp meeting. They were having a great time that evening. They were singing, and when I got there, they were singing a song that isn't very high-class music but has a lot of good doctrine in it—"I Feel Like Traveling On" (attributed to William Hunter, n.d.). They must have felt like traveling, because they sang about ten verses. Then they sat down, and an old lady got up again, and they all stood up and sang some more. I thought, *This crowd is going some place tonight. They really want to travel. We ought to feel like traveling on, because we're strangers and we're pilgrims; we're headed somewhere else.*

You were made for a better world, and you'll never be satisfied in this one. A dog is happy down here and satisfied because this is the only world the dog will ever know. But you're made for another one, and you just can't make yourself at home in this world. People try to make themselves happy and "at home" in this world. They get their split-level house out in suburbia, their cookout grill in the backyard, a boat, and all kind of paraphernalia, and they still are not happy. You just can't settle down in this world. If that's all you've got, you can't be happy, because you were made for another place. You're a transient; you're not a permanent. And we've been saved out of where we are now at.

Notice in John 17:11 that we're still in this world, even though we have been saved out of the world. We still have to live here physically. We live in its houses and ride on its trains and planes and trade in its stores and go to its schools and mix with its people. That's what Christians are supposed to do. You're no good isolated. The ancient mystics back in the early centuries of the church thought they made themselves holier by hiding in a hole in the ground, but you don't become holier by hiding in a hole somewhere. We've been saved to minister in this world, indeed. But the secret of it is found in John 17:15, where our Lord prayed, "I pray not that thou shouldest take them out of the world, but that thou shouldest keep them from the evil." Jesus means, "I'm not asking you to take them home to heaven, but to take them through."

Parents pray like that for their children: "Lord, don't take them out; take them through." And He can, and He will. I think my old father must have prayed that prayer for me. We used to hear Dad praying at night. He seemed to pray all hours of the night. I used to wonder when he slept. He was praying for us. And I think the burden of his prayer often must have been, "Lord, don't take them out; take them through." And He can.

My Lord was in this world. He was not a recluse or a hermit. He went to the weddings. He mixed with the publicans and sinners. The Pharisees, those folks who were separated from sinners but not from sin, criticized him. Our Lord associated with the world, but He never had fellowship with it. All right, we've been saved out of it. We're still in it. Look at verses 14 and 16, and at what's repeated; our Lord says in verse 14, "They are not of the world, even as I am not of the world." Verse 16 says, "They are not of the world, even as I am not of the world." When the boat's in the water, that's one thing; but when the water's in the boat, that's something else again.

We're not to be conformed to this world (see Rom. 12:2). We're to keep ourselves unspotted. We're to have no fellowship with the unfruitful works of darkness. "Love not the world, neither the things that are in the world. If any man love the world, the love of the Father is not in him" (1 John 2:15). This is what the Bible calls worldliness: "The lust of the flesh, and the lust of the eyes, and the pride of life, is not of the Father, but is of the world. And the world passeth away, and the lust thereof: but he that doeth the will of God abideth for ever" (vv. 16b–17). John had so much to say in both his Gospel and letters. John quotes our Lord much with references to this world (e.g., John 3:19; 7:7; 8:23; 9:39; 12:25).

There's a lot of confusion today about worldliness. I have heard preachers confine their remarks to card playing, dancing, going to the movies, and two or three other things. You got the idea that that is worldliness, and when you cover that territory you have exhausted the subject. There's a lot of worldliness that doesn't get in a thousand miles of that. What is worldliness? Well, my Lord said, "As it was in the days of [Noah], so shall it be also in the days of the Son of man" (Luke 17:26). How was it then? "They did eat, they drank, they married wives, they were given in marriage, until the day that [Noah] entered into the ark" (v. 27a). Now there's nothing wrong with those things in themselves. But when it's all that you do, or when you do it to the neglect of God and your own soul, then you are occupied with this age. That is worldliness. I'm thinking of a farmer who raises hogs. That's all he does. He's giving his life to raising hogs, a terrible thing to live for. I've heard of folks "going to the dogs"; he's gone to the hogs. But his real problem is that he has no time for God.

Did you ever stand on a street corner and just listen to people talk and try to guess what they're talking about? I'll guarantee that nine out of ten of them will be talking about some form of eating and drinking, marrying and giving in marriage, buying and selling, planting and doing. That's what people live for. And when it's all that you live for, it's worldliness, whether you ever do any of these things that we preach against or not. So the Bible says we are to deny ungodliness and the lusts of this age.

Some of this worldliness may be very refined. It may even be religious. But righteousness has no fellowship with unrighteousness. Light has no communion with darkness. He that believes has no part with an infidel, and a temple of God has no agreement with idols. And Christ has no symphony with Belial (see 2 Cor. 6:15). In your King James the word is "concord," and that's the Latinish form. But the original word is the word from which we get a musical term *symphony*. All kinds of symphonies have been written. This is the *impossible symphony*. What *symphony*, what *harmony*, what *concord* has Christ with Belial? The issue today, my friends, is not "wars and rumors of wars" nor "the number of wars and rumors of wars" nor the sagging economy. The issue today is just what it always has been—Christ or Antichrist. You can't serve two masters, God and mammon; Christ and this world.

We're hearing some strange things today in evangelical circles. We're reading in religious magazines that we ought to hobnob with Sodom and Gomorrah and get chummy with this age in order to reach it, that the end justifies the means. It's all right, they say, for a converted nightclub singer to stay in the nightclub as long as she winds up the program singing, "I'd Rather Have Jesus." At that rate, I expect one of these days to meet a Christian pickpocket. And when I ask him, "How do you do it?" He'll say, "Well, while I pick one pocket, I put a gospel tract in the other pocket." That's no more foolish than some of the means that are being justified by the goal of evangelism. The late-nineteenth-century English expositor Alexander Maclaren said, "The measure of our discord with the world is the measure of our accord with the Savior." And Gypsy Smith, who was a revival evangelist for seventy years, said, "If you are in with God, you are at odds with this world." Notice the contrast in John 17:14a: "I have given them thy word, and the world hated them." We choose between the Word or the world, for they're at odds with each other.

In John 7:3–4, Jesus' brother told Him to go up to Jerusalem and perform. "Get out of the backwoods. No one will ever see you out here. Get up there before the people." Jesus answered, "The world cannot hate you; but me it hateth, because I testify of it, that the works thereof are evil" (v. 7). Any preacher who testifies against worldliness will be the object of the hatred of this world. Jesus said, "It can't hate you, but it does hate me." Then He said in John 15:18–19, "If the world hate you, ye know that it hated me before it hated you. If ye were of the world, the world would love his own: but because ye are not of the world, but I have chosen you out of the world, therefore the world hateth you" (vv. 18–19). Now that forever blows to smithereens any acceptance of worldliness that has crept into evangelical Christianity. You are hated of this age if you take your stand with Jesus Christ. I don't mean that you can't be respected. I don't mean that you can't be looked up to with regard by many, but you can't be popular. First John 3:1 says, "The world knoweth us not, because it knew him not."

We Baptists are supposed to believe in the separation of church and state, and we may and we ought. But, really, I don't think a revival would ever start over separation of church and state. I can tell you what would start one, though—if Christians would wake up to separation of the church and the world. Now that might start something. And I wish some of our Southern Baptists could get as excited over the separation of the church and the world as they have over separation of church and state. While both are worthy, to be sure, I don't perceive much agitation lately over the second. And then, they say, you have to compromise with the world in order to influence it.

I heard of a preacher who had taken a new pastorate. Some in his congregation wanted him to join all the clubs in town, but he didn't feel inclined to do it. One rainy day he was driving along on the highway and passed by where the car of one of his deacons had skidded off into the mud. And the preacher said, "I'll back down into there and pull you out." The deacon said, "Oh, no, you stay up there. If you get down here, we'll both be stuck in the mud." That's just what the preacher was waiting for. He said, "Now that's what you've been wanting me to do spiritually. Ever since I came to this town, you've been wanting me to leave the King's highway and back off into every mud puddle of this world on the pretext of pulling somebody else out."

It's all right to throw out a tow chain, but you stay on the King's highway.

Finally, my Lord says in John 17:18, that we've been saved out of the world. We're still in the world. We're not of the world, but we've been saved out of the world. "As thou hast sent me into the world, even so have I also sent them into the world." We have been saved out of this world to go right back into the world to win people out of the world, and that's the only business we have in this world. That's the Christian's business here. We're not here to adopt the world system. We're not here to be conformed to it. We're not here to sit in judgment and look down our noses at it in pharisaic super-sanctity. We're not here to boast of our self-righteousness, that we don't do this and we don't do that. I've known these super saints in some churches who wrap the rags of their self-righteousness around themselves just because they don't dance or smoke or play cards. They glory in that "I don't do these things." I feel like saying, "Well, neither does a gate post."

What *are you doing* to the glory of God? It's not just a matter of what you don't do. It's possible not to do this and not to do that, but still be covetous and a tattler and a backbiter and be jealous and take God's name in vain and follow a dozen evil practices of disposition that are just as loathsome. The real issue is that it's not a matter of quitting this and quitting that. It's a matter of telling this old world good-bye, once and for all. And when you've done it, include everything that is

wrong, whatever your particular temptations may be. The
Lord saved us to send us right back out into this world to be a
light in the dark place. They don't need a light in an illumi-
nated place; they need a light in the dark place.

In John 17:19a, Jesus says, "For their sakes I sanctify myself." Suppose you went into an operating room, and the surgeons and nurses were dressed in dirty garments. They had
not washed their hands nor sterilized the instruments. When
you complain, they say, "The only thing that matters is our
position. Our condition doesn't matter, just our position. We're
surgeons and nurses. See our diplomas?" That's not enough.
Some Christians say, "I'm a Christian. I've been saved, but I
don't worry too much about how I live. My condition doesn't
matter so much." Yes, it does. "Be ye holy; for I am holy" (1 Peter 1:16). We ought to be holy for God's sake.

Years ago I was in a meeting in a Georgia town. About the
second night of the meeting, the young pastor of the church
came under the conviction of the Holy Spirit about something he was doing. Plenty of preachers do that. But he came
to me after the service and said, "I feel convicted about this
matter." He said, "I have confessed it. I have put it away, but
do you think I ought to say anything to my people tomorrow
night about it?" And I told him, "We're not running a meeting where we just do anything we feel like, but if the Lord
leads you to make a public statement, you do whatever the
Spirit guides you to do." He got up the next night and made a
forthright statement.

He became one of our foremost missionaries in South
America and has been there for a long time. He said in a Bible
conference some years ago, "It was when Brother Havner was
with me in a meeting, the Lord spoke to me afresh." He had
already yielded his life to the Lord, but there was a sin that

was capturing his attention. But when he turned that sin over to God, God helped him get his priorities in order. He said the verse that had blessed him was the Word of our Lord, "Wherefore come out from among them, and be ye separate, saith the Lord, and touch not the unclean thing; and I will receive you, and will be a Father unto you" (2 Cor. 6:17–18a). Look what God had accomplished through this man in South America. It all hinged, really, on what he did about one sinful habit.

There may be a similar sinful habit or problem that has you tangled in the world. If you, like this young man, will say good-bye to the things of this world and commit yourself to walking with the Lord, there's no telling where the Lord may lead you in His service. There's one thing for certain; you can't walk two roads at the same time.

Chapter 9

IF WE HAD REVIVAL

*O*n the day of Pentecost, when the multitudes saw the early church filled with the Spirit, they asked, "What meaneth this?" (Acts 2:12). You remember that Peter replied, "This is that which was spoken by the prophet Joel" (v. 16). And after his sermon, his listeners asked, "What shall we do? What does this mean? This is that? Then, what shall we do?" We have tried to reverse the order today. We expect the world to ask, "What shall we do?" But they've not seen enough going on in the churches to make them ask first, "What does this mean?" In our desperation, we've put on religious extravaganzas and stirred religious excitements and simulated religious ecstasies. But the multitude is not crying out, "What shall we do?"

We're living in a day of Jesus movements and charismatic movements and great religious gatherings, when "Amazing Grace" is a bestseller and gospel rock packs the auditoriums and the name of Jesus is at an all-time high of popularity, whatever that means. And from every direction, people are asking, "Is this revival? Are we having a spiritual awakening?"

The question is its own answer, because it raises doubt and uncertainty. If we ever have a real revival again, we'll know it. A genuine work of God is always self-authenticated. It bears its own credentials, and you won't need a conference of experts to identify it.

There are certain marks of revival. If we were having it, there would be a return to the authority of the Bible as the inerrant inspiration and the Word of God. Some of the brethren battling for orthodoxy today ought to wager on calling the church to repentance, because when the church repents and forsakes its doubt, liberalism doesn't have a leg to stand on. And the revival that argument could never accomplish comes naturally, or I should say, supernaturally, when men turn to God. R. B. Jones wrote in his book *Rent Heavens* (2d ed., 1948) that one newspaper during the great Welsh Revival in 1904–5 said, "The revival is largely a protest against the philosophic Christianity that was preached by the ministers whom the Welsh University colleges had trained." Another paper said one minister greatly used in the revival had been interested in higher criticism and a new theology, but he had a new experience, and the writings of the higher critics lost their attraction for him.

The revival released many from the grip of religious heterodoxy. Orthodoxy itself needs a revival today. Along with a return to sound doctrine, we must get back to spiritual renewal within, or we don't have a revival. Nothing is deader than the dead orthodoxy of cold fundamentalism. Pharisees were orthodox, but their hearts were not right, and they drew our Lord's most severe condemnation. The greatest enemies my Lord had on earth were not the bums and bootleggers and criminals. His worst opposition came from folks who went to church, read the Bible, prayed in public, tithed, lived moral lives separated from the world, tried to win others, and were headed to hell. You can have all kinds of points with religion and not be a Christian. Jesus said, "The publicans and the harlots go into the kingdom of God before you," (Matt. 21:31b). And He said that "except your righteousness shall exceed the righteousness of the scribes and Pharisees, ye shall in no case enter into the kingdom of heaven" (5:20).

If we were having revival today, there would be a profound conviction of sin (which I don't see much of), confession of sin, and forsaking sin. We've given the sin issue new names today. We call it "immaturity, arrested development, biological growing pains, and error of mortal mind." God has become "the big buddy upstairs." Parents no longer use the word *lost.* I don't know when I last heard a father or mother say, "My boy or girl is lost." I used to hear parents cry out for their children. Now they say, "Well, my Johnny is a good boy." The rich young ruler was a *good boy,* but he wasn't *God's boy.* Depravity today is largely a matter of complexes and inhibitions. We leave it for the psychiatrists and not the preacher. Old-fashioned sinners are harder to find today than whooping cranes. I don't hear many prodigals saying, "I have sinned." We call fornication "pre-marital sex," and adultery is just "an affair."

Many think nothing of taking the name of God in vain. You don't have to cuss to do that. You can stand in church and sing, "Have Thine Own Way, Lord." If you don't mean it, you've taken God's name in vain. But taking God's name in vain has become so common that nobody lifts an eyebrow.

I listened to a discussion the other day by prominent figures on television of matters that nobody ever discussed before except husband and wife in their own bedroom. Yet frank sexuality is getting to be common vernacular. We cannot expect God to take away our sins by forgiving them if we're not willing to put them away by forsaking them. The Bible says, "He that covereth his sins shall not prosper: but whoso confesseth and forsaketh them shall have mercy" (Prov. 28:13). It isn't enough to confess your sins. You must not only ask God to take them away. You must put them away. There will be no mercy and forgiveness until the wicked forsake their ways and the unrighteous their thoughts.

If we were having revival, the divorce rate would drop and houses would become homes again, marriage would be for life, unwed college students wouldn't be living like man and wife in dormitories, and pornography and nudity and homosexuality and other abominations that are now accepted wouldn't be acceptable. A man would take his place as head of the home, and a woman would be the heart of the home, as it used to be. Any home with two heads and no heart is a monstrosity. Whatever women's lib would think of such a movement, it would restore discipline that has disappeared almost entirely from the home and church. Husbands and wives would get along.

Two married folks were in the rest home. The old man thought he'd say something nice to his wife. He said, "I'm proud of you."

She said, "Eh?"

"I said, 'I'm proud of you.'"

"I didn't hear you."

"I said, 'I'm proud of you.'"

She said, "I'm tired of you, too."

An awful lot of folks are tired of their spouses today. Are you tired of her? Are you tired of him? I tell you, if we ever have revival, we'll learn to love each other in all relationships of life as we should.

There'd be an impact on lawlessness and crime. It's as if the highway department has torn down all the highway signs and left everybody to their own judgment. The lenient courts give the criminal just a slight little reprimand. Infested by the demonized denizens of darkness, the streets are no longer safe for decent citizens. And if we took crimes against each other seriously, there would be reconciliation and restitution among Christians. We would confess our own faults one to another. It doesn't take much religion to confess other people's faults. My Lord said, "If thou bring thy gift to the altar, and there rememberest that thy brother hath aught against thee; leave there thy gift before the altar, and go thy way; first be reconciled to thy brother, and then come and offer thy gift" (Matt. 5:23–24). Before you bring your envelope to church or your offering, get right with your brother.

Churches are rent today, even conservative orthodox fundamental churches, with the sins that Paul enumerated: envying, strife, division, swellings, whispering, tumults, schisms, variants, debates, contentions, tattling, gossiping, backbiting, and jealousy (2 Cor. 12:20). Husbands and wives, parents and children, and neighbors ought to be reconciled. There are personality clashes on church staffs—sins of tongue, and sins of temper. Zacchaeus needs to come down out of that sycamore tree and straighten his crooked business practices (see Luke 19:1–9). And we still have those hypocrites my Lord blasted when He said, "For ye devour widows' houses, and for a pretence make long prayer" (Matt. 23:14).

A revival would mean a decline of worldliness in the church. I don't hear the word *worldliness* anymore. Now it is called "secularism." Nobody knows what that means, so the preacher is off the hook. He doesn't have to preach on worldliness. But my Bible says, "Come out from among them, and be ye separate" (2 Cor. 6:17). Today, even for conservative Christians, anything that sounds like separation from the world is abhorred as though it were the bubonic plague. As the age draws to its close and Babylon shakes up and the harlot rides the beast, the world and the church have been casting eyes at each other, falling in love. The wedding approaches.

There was a day when preachers thundered out against specific sins. They tell us today, "Don't deal in the negatives. Don't deal in the wicked things people are doing." When Jesus talked to the woman at Jacob's well, he talked about worship, and he talked about the water of life, but that woman was not under conviction until He became specific. "Go, call thy husband" (John 4:16). That's where the trouble was. She'd had too many of them. It's not enough to preach on sin. We must name something. Some folks will get mad, but they are not going to come under conviction by generalizations. They are convicted when the Spirit of God through the Word of God names something. Churches now are revising their covenants. I know of a big church that took out all references to any specific sin and put in its place "all evil." That leaves everybody free to decide what they think is evil.

When we have revival, we'll fix our eyes on Jesus, and the things of earth will grow strangely dim. There'll be an outbreak of old-fashioned, original New Testament Christianity. The professing church wavers today between two extremes, *rigor mortis* on one side and Saint Vitus's dance [a once-popular term describing body jerks brought on by the disease Huntington chorea] on the other. We are living in a Christless Christianity, a lukewarm Laodesianism on one side, and on the other a churchless Christianity among those who reject all organized expressions of the church. Jesus loved the church and gave Himself for it. He's the groom, and the church is the bride. You're not going to have much of a wedding with a brideless groom and a groomless bride. He's the head, and the church is the body. I'm not interested in a headless body or a bodiless head.

If a revival were going on, there'd be a radical change. Old-fashioned New Testament Christianity would return.

A. W. Tozer of the Christian Missionary Alliance said, "The present flare for religion has not made people more heavenly minded. It has secularized religion, has glorified success, and eagerly prints religious testimonials from big corporation tycoons, actors, athletes, politicians, and very important persons of every kind, regardless of their reputation, or lack of one." Religion is promoted by the same techniques used to sell cigarettes. You pray to soothe your nerves just as you smoke to regain your composure. Books are written to show that Jesus is a regular fellow, and Christianity is just a wise use of the high psychological laws. The meek are not blessed, but the self-important. It is not those who mourn who are blessed, but they that smile and smile and smile. It is not the poor in spirit who are deemed dear to God, but those who are accounted significant by the secular press.

If a revival were going on, we'd be delivered from such popular aberrations as the notion that we must dress like the world and talk like the world and sing like the world in order to reach it for Christ. You don't have to look like a clown to witness to a circus.

I was pastor of the First Baptist Church of Charleston, South Carolina, from 1934 to 1939. This is the oldest Baptist church in the South. It was organized in 1683. Every Saturday night while I was there, I'd go to the rescue mission to preach. I didn't dress like a bum to make my ministry effective. Even the bums, I think, would have resented that. You don't have to look like the world to reach the world. They tell us today that we must use the new terminology, that we must be relevant and communicate and have rapport, whatever that is, and that we must study the spectrum, and we must get down to the nitty-gritty. Forget it. They used to call it an "itch," and now they call it an "allergy," but you scratch just the same.

If revival were going on, there'd be a recovery of modest dress and deportment. Christians would be different in appearance and set a standard for a sex-crazy generation. I know that they say it's not a matter of what you wear, but rather the state of your heart. But the world doesn't see your heart. It sees your clothes, and it sees you. I didn't expect many amens from that part of the sermon. There's no evidence of freakishness in the appearance of Jesus. He set no weird standards in haberdashery or haircuts. If revival were going on, Christians would attract no special attention either way, but certainly they would be clean and neat and look their best for the glory of God. Paul told Timothy to look out for three trends. First is the peril of things. The love of money is the root of all kinds of evil (1 Tim. 6:10). Second, Paul said to look for perils concerning the times (see 2 Tim. 3:1–9). In the last days, perilous times will come, perils concerning the truth. Third, men will turn from the truth to fables (4:4). The best way to judge anything that you've got any doubt about is to ask which way it is going, not where it is right now. It may not be bad right now. But ask yourself where you will go if you go with it? We must nip these things in the bud. I know they are only symptoms and not the disease. But any doctor will tell you that symptoms are important. They indicate what the disease may be.

If we were having revival, the sanctity of the Lord's Day would be restored. What used to be the Lord's Day is now the "weekend." Long holidays and four-day work weeks have torn up the picture so that churches are having a rough time. If we extend leisure much longer, I wonder what will happen. Look at the way most people spend their leisure time. One of our major Protestant traditions in its statement about the Lord's Day says that we should refrain from all secular employment except works of necessity and works of mercy (*Westminster Confession of Faith*). Well, that's all right. Sunday football hardly qualifies as a work of necessity, and it certainly is not a work of mercy. If all the preachers and the parishioners whose eyes are glued to Sunday afternoon television were on their knees in repentance and prayer, the revival would be a lot nearer.

Early in church history holy days became mixed with pagan holidays because so many pagans after Constantine became professing Christians. He made it fashionable to be a Christian. Everybody started joining church, and that nearly ruined Christianity. And in order to make Christianity more acceptable to these heathen church members, they mixed the holidays and the holy days. That's why Christmas is all tangled up with Santa Claus, and Easter with bunny rabbits and eggs. We'll never get it untangled. The church moved from the catacombs under the ground to the Colosseum where the prizefights were held, and we lost ground we've never regained.

There was a day when preachers like Sam Jones and Billy Sunday fought the liquor business. Today, even religious leaders sometimes have a good word for cocktails. And Paul's advice to Timothy about drinking a little wine for your stomach's sake is one of the most overworked verses I know of in the New Testament. I look for a great outbreak of stomach trouble among Baptists during the next few years. It is ridiculous to hear these TV discussions on the problem of alcoholism, as experts try to find out what causes it. I'm from the hills of Western North Carolina and there are a lot of things I don't know, but I always thought the cause of alcoholism was alcohol. I think that makes sense. Now we're trying to mop up the floor leaving the faucet running, trying to sweep out the cobwebs and never touch the spider. We must do something about it. We must face the issue. This smiling tolerance from the pulpit is a concession to the cocktail drinkers and the country clubbers and the potential alcoholics in the congregation.

Now if we were really having revival, it would follow the context of the text that Peter used at Pentecost. Few know anything in the book of Joel except that one text Peter used. Joel was a revivalist. He said, "Blow the trumpet in Zion, sanctify a fast, call a solemn assembly" (Joel 2:15). Then he called for everybody to repent. This wasn't a youth revival. This was for everybody:

> Gather the people, sanctify the congregation, assemble the elders, gather the children, and those that suck the breasts: let the bridegroom go forth of his chamber, and the bride out of her closet. Let the priests, the ministers of the LORD, weep between the porch and the altar, and let them say, Spare thy people, O LORD, and give not thine heritage to reproach, that the heathen should rule over them: wherefore should they say among the people, Where is their God? (vv. 16–17)

Joel said, "Lord, I'm tired of the world going by saying, 'Where is your God? Where is the God of Abraham and Isaac and Jacob? Where is He?'" The world asks those questions today, but we're embarrassed to answer. In Joel, all ages were called upon to repent. Those familiar verses we know come after repentance. After repentance old men and young men will dream dreams and see visions and all the rest. All ages will rejoice if all ages will repent (see Joel 2:28–32). When we meet the conditions, God will pour out His blessing.

The question is asked, "Will there again be a great outpouring of the Spirit?" The Scriptures teach that the age will end in anarchy, apostasy, and apathy—*anarchy* in the world, *apostasy* in the professing church, and even *apathy* in the true church—because lawlessness shall abound, the love of most will wax cold (see Matt. 24:12). Men will turn from the truth to fables. "When the Son of man cometh, shall he find faith on the earth?" (Luke 18:8). There may be a quickening of the remnant, but the world goes hurtling on toward destruction. Pentecost didn't save Jerusalem from judgment. The Spirit is always working. He's working today in faithful Christians and Bible conferences and revivals and New Testament churches and among a lot of our young people. But there's no mighty awakening that produces such evidence as I named at the beginning. And I'm more afraid of a false revival today than I am of no revival. We're in great danger of one that's going to look so much like the real thing that a lot of good people will be fooled. The Devil is the great imitator. He does more harm as an angel of light than he ever did as a roaring lion. When Moses performed his wonders, Jannes and Jambres were ready to perform a counterfeit. And the Devil scatters the tares among the wheat, and nobody but the angels will know the difference. There's a wave of simulated religion going around today. Even good people are afraid to say anything about it. The sin against the Holy Spirit lay in ascribing the work of God to the Devil. But today, we're ascribing the work of the Devil to God. If revival comes in the providence of God, you'll never regulate it like a stopwatch. You can't regulate the Holy Spirit. He's sovereign. One thing is certain, it's not going to come until the church repents. Repentance is the blind spot in our eyes today.

Whether we ever have a great revival, we can set our own house in order. You can say, "As for me and my house, we will serve the Lord" (Josh. 24:15c). You can "gird up the loins of your mind" (1 Pet. 1:13) and "stir up the gift of God" (2 Tim. 1:6) and renew the covenant and walk with the Lord in the light of His Word and reckon yourself dead to sin and alive to God (see Rom. 6:1–8) and redeem the time because the days are evil (Eph. 5:16). Whatever other people do, you can be faithful. But today we're getting away from setting our house in order.

I close as I began. When real revival comes, we'll know it. I think of the great Shantung revival in China.

I used to think that a revival started among the backsliders, the Christmas and Easter crowd, the Sunday morning glories that bloom on Sunday morning and fold up for the rest of the week. I thought that's who you had to start with. Oh, no. Revival starts with the best people. It starts with deacons. It starts with the Sunday school teachers.

The Shantung revival started with Hugo H. Culpepper, who was one of the saintliest men that ever went to China. When God got through dealing with him, you'd have thought he was the worst sinner over there. A missionary was holding meetings, and she'd stand at the door as everybody went out to ask each, "Have you been born again?" She asked Dr. Culpepper, "Have you ever been filled with the Spirit?" He hemmed and hawed and swallowed and hardly knew what to say, good man as he was. God used that missionary lady to start a work in Culpepper. It starts with the best people. If you're going to build a fire, you don't start with the backlog, but with kindling wood. God wants to gather a little kindling. That's what I'm doing today everywhere I go, gathering a few people who will start something for the Lord.

All over this land I see people straining and striving, red in the face and puffing, trying to make revival. I think we've missed the point. God said to Joshua when he lay on his face, "Get up" (see Josh. 7:6–15). This was not the time for a prayer meeting. I've been in prayer meetings that were a waste of time because the people wouldn't face sin. God told Joshua that Israel had sinned, and he had to deal with that. Somebody's got to confess sin. When people are purified, Jesus says, "He that drinketh of this water, from within him shall flow rivers of living water."

All the wonderful things you read about in the Acts of the Apostles were simply the outflow and the overflow of the inflow of the Spirit of God—just that. When you get the debris out of the way, the water of life will flow, and we'll have revival.

Chapter 10

JESUS IS LORD

For we preach not ourselves, but Christ Jesus the Lord;
and ourselves your servants for Jesus' sake. (2 Cor. 4:5)

*S*econd Corinthians 4:5 tells us what the apostle
Paul did *not* preach and what we *are* to preach. I like the tri-
angle in the last half of that verse: "ourselves your servants for
Jesus' sake."

If I were to ask you, "Do you believe in the Lordship of
Jesus Christ?" you would probably answer very comfortably
that you do. But if I were to come around and ask you one by
one, "Is He your Lord, Lord of all you have and do?" what
would you say? Any congregation can sing "Bring forth the
royal diadem and crown Him Lord of all" (Edward Perronet,
"All Hail the Power of Jesus Name," 1779). But not all who are
willing to crown Him with their lips are ready to obey Him in
their lives.

Samuel Taylor Coleridge said, "There are some truths that
are regarded as so true that they lose the power of truth and
lie bedridden in the dormitory of the soul." And there are some
things that we've heard so much and so often, they don't move
us anymore; they lie inoperative in the dormitories of our
minds. One of these is the lordship of Christ. The word *lord* is
one of the most lifeless words in the Christian vocabulary, yet
A. T. Robertson called the lordship of Christ "the touchstone

of the Christian faith." G. Campbell Morgan called it "the central verity of the church." A continuous problem that society deals with is authority versus anarchy. In the time of the judges, "there was no king in Israel: every man did that which was right in his own eyes" (Judg. 21:25; cf. 17:6). There was no authority, so every man did as he pleased—anarchy. When authority goes out, anarchy comes in.

Our Lord told us that in the last days lawlessness would abound, and Paul writes of the mystery of lawlessness that leads up to antichrist (2 Thess. 2:7). All the misery recorded in the book of Judges was due to mistakes recorded in the book of Joshua, mistakes made when Israel took the promised land. They were told to exterminate the inhabitants, and they didn't. I think I know what happened. They won a few battles, and then I think they said, "I'm getting tired of fighting; I'm getting tired of getting up every morning and taking off for a battle. These Canaanites aren't such bad people. Let's have a little peaceful coexistence." Peace without victory; one way or another we've been trying to have that ever since. You know what happened. The conquerors became the conquered, and the victors became the victims.

In America, we tried peaceful coexistence with communism. We tried it at first with Nazism under Adolf Hitler and found out you couldn't do business with Hitler. Then we tried peaceful coexistence with Josef Stalin, and it still didn't work, because communism is like cancer: you do not peacefully coexist with cancer. If you don't get the cancer, the cancer gets you. General Douglas MacArthur stood before the U.S. Congress and said, "In war, there is no substitute for victory." In the 1960s, the Israeli-Arab war was won in a hurry because, as the top general of Israel said, "We had one element that we don't think any other nation has—no alternative. We had to win.

We couldn't fight a long war. We couldn't fight a stalemate. We had to win." It would be a fine thing if we could get some of God's people to go about holy warfare that way. Well, as a consequence of this denial of authority, we have anarchy in all realms.

I saw in the Birmingham, Alabama, newspaper a picture painted by an ape. He had rubbed his nose in various paint jars and then rubbed his nose on the paper. Of course, I'm not surprised that an ape can do that. This is anarchy in modern art. Our world is an asylum, run by the inmates. On TV we see world events that are not ordinary wickedness. It is not run-of-the-mill meanness that we read about now. It is demonism.

The Ten Commandments have been thrown out the window, and now we have situation ethics and context immorality. Right and wrong are relative, not absolute. "It all depends on how you look at it." No, it doesn't. It depends on what God says about it in His Word. While on a summertime picnic, a boy stole a watermelon from a patch nearby. His mother scolded, "Now don't do that again. You don't know what they've been sprayed with." See what I mean? We live with not a word about the Ten Commandments, not a word about stealing. Many millions of dollars worth of goods are stolen each year by shoplifters. I'd hate to think how many church members were in that aggregation. This anarchy is even infecting the home. There's as much authority in the homes as ever. The difference is, the children use it. It has changed hands.

Anarchy extends to courts in which the criminal is given more sympathy than the victim. We treat hoodlums like daffodils while we tie the hands of policemen. A policeman used to be respected. Now he's a target for brickbats. Authority out, anarchy in.

It all boils down to the denial of the absolute sovereignty of Jesus Christ. Romans 14:9 says, "For to this end Christ both died, and rose, and revived, that he might be Lord both of the dead and living." And the day is coming when everybody in heaven, earth and under the earth shall confess Him as Lord. It won't save the lost, not then, but everybody will do it. All the anarchy, all the violence, all the war and the rioting and the looting and the crying occur because men and women refuse the lordship of Jesus Christ. We're wasting our time laying the blame on secondary issues and trying to solve problems by education, legislation, and reformation. You can give every disgruntled, dissatisfied, yelling maniac today a home in suburbia and two automobiles and a color TV and a boat and all the status he wants. Next week he'll be howling for something else until he bows, as bow he will in hell if not here, to the absolute lordship of Jesus Christ. But even those who accept Jesus as Savior often deny Him as Lord. Our personal problems and our church problems today boil down to the denial of the supreme lordship of Christ.

Christians are living in an inner anarchy. Some things I'm reading today even in evangelical papers appall me. We're getting away from the total authority of the Word of God. Old-fashioned standards of morality and honesty and purity and modesty have been thrown out the window. I know some people say all that stuff is "old fogyism." I looked up that word *fogy* in the dictionary. A fogy is, "a person of old-fashioned habits." Well what's wrong with that? What's wrong with purity and morality and honesty and modesty? We have anarchy in conservative Christianity—strife, division, schism, debates, variants, contingents. We have a breakdown in separation from the world. Christians smile indulgently at the fashions of this age—clothes and conduct, dress and deportment.

In our music, we've come all the way from hymns to hoote-nannies, and church discipline is a thing of the past. The trend is toward anarchy, away from authority, the authority of Jesus Christ as Lord. *First, the lordship of Christ was the initial confession of the church.* "That if thou shalt confess with thy mouth the Lord Jesus, and shalt believe in thine heart that God hath raised him from the dead, thou shalt be saved" (Rom. 10:9). When an early Christian man said, "Jesus is Lord," he meant it; he'd better mean it. A Jewish believer had better mean it, for *Lord* meant *Jehovah*. A Gentile in the Roman Empire had better mean it because Caesar was the only emperor, and some em-perors in the first century aspired to godhood as well. A Chris-tian was in a lot of trouble if he said, "I have another king, and my total allegiance is to Him." All through the New Testa-ment, beloved, it's never "Christ and. . . ." You don't add any-thing to Jesus. He's Alpha and Omega and all the letters between. When you write a letter to someone, you don't have to search outside the alphabet for letters to use. Everything you need is there. Jesus said concerning the hungry multi-tude, "They need not depart; give ye them to eat" (Matt. 14:16; cf. Mark 6:37a; Luke 9:13a). They don't have to go anywhere else. We have what they need. Let's get the food out. "Give ye them to eat."

Early Christianity demanded a clean break with the world, the flesh, and the Devil, and that lasted until Constantine be-came a church member and tried to Christianize paganism and wound up "paganizing" Christianity. The church tried to control the culture. It was "Constantinized" but not Chris-tianized. We have never gotten over that mistake, the mistake of Constantine. And to this day, although Nero is dead, too many church members try to serve two lords. Our churches have been filled with baptized pagans living double lives—fearing the Lord and serving their own gods, drawing nigh God with their mouths and honoring Him with their lips while their hearts are far from Him, calling Him "Lord, Lord," and not doing what He says.

Second, the Lordship of Christ is the authentic confession of a Christian. "Wherefore I give you to understand, that no man speaking by the Spirit of God calleth Jesus accursed: and that no man can say that Jesus is the Lord, but by the Holy Ghost" (1 Cor. 12:3). You cannot confess Jesus as Lord by yourself. You can't save yourself. You can't understand the Bible by yourself. These things require the operation of the Holy Spirit. It's not a do-it-yourself religion. You can call Him Lord and not mean it. Jesus said there would be those at the judgment who would say, "Lord, Lord, have we not prophesied in thy name? and in thy name have cast out devils? and in thy name done many wonderful works? And then will I profess unto them, I never knew you: depart from me" (Matt. 7:22–23). Luke 6:46 says, "And why call ye me, Lord, Lord, and do not the things which I say?" But it is an authentic mark of the work of the Holy Spirit to truly confess Jesus as Lord, for the old Adam never bows to the lordship of Jesus Christ.

I think we preachers have unwittingly created an artificial distinction between accepting Jesus as Savior and confessing Him as Lord. We've made two things out of it, and it's not two things; it's all one thing. A great many people today have the idea that, "I can take the free part, salvation. I'll take Jesus as Savior. I don't want to go to hell. I'll take Jesus as Savior. I'll not take Him as Lord now. I'll think it over, and maybe sometime at a dedication meeting I'll go forward and take Him as Lord. In the meantime, if I never do, I'll go to heaven anyhow. The only thing I'll lose will be my reward." That's very strange doctrine. It certainly isn't New Testament doctrine. Salvation is not a cafeteria line where you go along and take what you want and leave the rest. You don't get saved on the installment plan with your fingers crossed and inner reservations. You can't take Jesus on approval like you buy a stock of goods. To be sure, we may not understand all that's involved. And all the rest of our lives, fresh areas are opening up that need to be subjected to the lordship of Christ. If we take Jesus for all we know Him to be at that time, God will save us. We don't have to be theologians. But no one can take Jesus as Savior and at the same time willfully and deliberately and knowingly refuse Him as Lord, and be saved.

Paul said to the Philippian jailer, "Believe on the Lord Jesus Christ, and thou shalt be saved" (Acts 16:31). He gave Him all three names at once: Master, Mediator, and Messiah. He didn't say, "Now, you make a profession of faith, and we'll take you in the church, put your name on the roll, and give you a box of envelopes, and you'll be all right." He said, "Let's have it over, all of it, at the start, 'lock, stock, and barrel.'" You have only one choice in this world. You can take Christ or not take Him, but if you ever take Him, friend, your option ends right there. From then on, you become the personal property of Jesus Christ, bought and paid for by His blood. You're not your own. You're bought with a price. Jesus Christ demanded more absolute loyalty than any dictator—Charlemagne, Caesar, Hitler. None of these ever demanded the absolute allegiance that Jesus demands, but He has a right to. "Love so amazing, so divine, demands my soul, my life, my all" (Isaac Watts, "When I Survey the Wondrous Cross," 1707).

I remember when I came to Jesus as a country boy in old Catawba County out in the country while a revival was going on at Corinth Baptist Church in Vale, North Carolina. I wandered out in the woods one summer afternoon and trusted Jesus the best way I knew how. I didn't understand all about it. You don't have to "understand it all." You have to stand on it all. I don't understand all about electricity, but I'm not going to sit around in the dark until I do. I came to Jesus as I was—trusting. And that afternoon I was trying to do up the chores around the place and go back up to the service that night, and I was trying to sing that old song, "Jesus, I my cross have taken, all to leave and follow Thee" (Henry F. Lyte, "Jesus, I My Cross Have Taken," 1824). I haven't heard that in ages. This affluent society would have an awful time with that verse, wouldn't they? Can you imagine a well-fed, well-clothed, well-housed crowd of Americans standing up singing, "destitute, despised, forsaken, Thou from hence my all should be"? Lord, help us.

I didn't understand much about trusting Jesus, but I understood one thing. No theologian had to explain it to me. I understood that I was under new management. That was perfectly clear. I had a new Lord. I believe that the sad state of our Christians in churches today is due to a cheap *believism* that doesn't believe and a cheap *receivism* that doesn't receive. After all, the word *Savior* is found only 24 times in the New Testament, and the word *Lord* is applied to Jesus 433 times. He is Lord. A Christian is a believer, a disciple, and a witness. You ought to become all three at the same time and be all three all the rest of the time.

We were called "disciples" before we were ever called "Christians" (Acts 11:26). The Great Commission of Matthew 28:19–20 tells us to go and make disciples, not believers (Matt. 28:19). You have to be a believer to be a disciple, but let's get it straight: Make disciples. God's not out just saving sinners. He's out to make saints out of sinners. And the crisis of conversion must be followed by continuance. It's a great mistake to take a text that starts with the word *and*. I've seen on streamers and placards in the last few years, "And ye shall know the truth, and the truth shall make you free" (John 8:32). That's a good verse, but you wouldn't want to rise up in the middle of people who had never heard of Jesus Christ and just take off on that. You have two absolutes there. You have truth and freedom, but you'd have to get a head start. And, after all, that verse begins with the word *and*. That means something has gone before, and the verse before it is, "If ye continue in my word, then are ye my disciples indeed; and ye shall know the truth, and the truth shall make you free" (vv. 31–32). Don't you see what a difference that makes?

Oh, beloved, we've got to take not just a step but a walk and keep on stepping. Some dear folks say, "Well, I took a stand for the Lord twenty-five years ago," and some of them are still standing. We sing "Standing on the Promises" (R. Kelso Carter, c. 1886), but in truth we're sitting on the premises. We're not getting anywhere. You have to practice. You have to work at it. You have to learn of Him. We don't learn how to do anything else without plenty of practice. You don't learn how to be a musician, for instance, without practice.

I had meetings in a Texas city at which on this Sunday morning famous pianist Van Clyburn played the offertory. The children pressed him for an autograph, including yours truly. I had a chat with him in the pastor's study. He's a genius, yes; but genius isn't enough. The way that fellow practices would drive most people crazy: practice, practice, practice, practice. And when I think about the sloppy and slothful living patterns of most of our church members, I'm not surprised that we're not making much of a dent on this world today. People resent the preacher who stands in the pulpit and says, "Thou therefore endure hardness, as a good soldier of Jesus Christ" (2 Tim. 2:3).

At one time violin concerts were occasionally televised featuring the post-graduate classes of students of the masters. The students sounded perfect to me, but not to the masters. A master violinist might grumble, "There is no discipline. There is no discipline." I listened to that one evening, and I found myself praying, "Lord, have mercy on me when I think I'm pretty good. I want to be a workman, not ashamed, approved unto God." Are you a dropout? What does your report card look like? Are you anywhere near a post-graduate course? How is it with you, dear friend? You don't become a good Christian, you don't become a good soldier of the cross without working at it, just like you don't become a good acrobat without working at it.

Don Ameche says, "When acrobats are not performing, they're practicing." And that's just about it. They do only two things: practice and perform, practice and perform. You don't get up some morning and get a balancing rod in your hand and decide to take off on that tightwire. No, no. You'll take off all right, but you just don't learn that way. It takes infinite practice. And, beloved, it takes that in the discipleship of the Cross. When a child is born in a home, that's a great day. But it takes twenty years after that to make a man or a woman out of that child. Evangelism is great business, but it's only the beginning. Salvation is free; yes, but it's not cheap. It cost God plenty. It cost Him His Son. It cost the Son His life. It's free to you. But the minute you take it you become a disciple, and that will cost you everything you have. The New Testament teaches not only faith in Christ; it teaches following Christ. "My sheep hear my voice, and I know them, and they follow me" (John 10:27). "Come unto me" (Matt. 11:28a); that's for the believer. "Learn of me" (v. 29b); that's for the disciple. The believer comes to Christ; the disciple comes after that.

Peter followed my Lord from the Sea of Galilee. Then he denied Him one day, and for some days he was not a disciple. How do I know? Because the angel at the sepulchre said, "Go your way, tell his disciples and Peter" (Mark 16:7). Then Peter was reinstated by the Sea of Tiberius. We're great today for going after prospects in our churches. We're great prospectors. But did you ever stop to consider that Jesus lost some of His best prospects? And He did not lower any prices; He didn't take out after them and say, "Well, maybe we can talk this thing over and arrive at some kind of a compromise."

In Luke 9:57–62 are three fellows. As you remember, the first one said, "I will follow thee whithersoever thou goest" (v. 57), and Jesus said, "Foxes have holes, and birds of the air have nests; but the Son of man hath not where to lay his head" (v. 58). The second said, "Lord, suffer me first to go and bury my father" (v. 59). Jesus said, "Let the dead bury their dead: but go thou and preach the kingdom of God" (v. 60). The third said, "Lord, I will follow thee; but let me first go bid them farewell, which are at home at my house" (v. 61). Jesus said, "No man, having put his hand to the plough, and looking back, is fit for the kingdom of God" (v. 62). If you're going with me, let's go; if you're going to stay here, stay here; but the kingdom of God is no place for a man with his face pointed one way and his feet the other. God is not taking people to heaven backward. If you're going with me, let's get going, all in one direction.

One prospect, the rich young ruler, stood head and shoulders above the rest. He had manners, for he came very politely. He had morals. He kept the commandments. He had money. If he tried to join the average church today, they'd say, "Take him in quick. Make him treasurer and don't ask him any questions." My Lord said, "Sell out." He didn't give him a massage; He gave him a shock treatment. "Sell out," and that's just what he wouldn't do. He was a good catch, but the Lord didn't catch him. My Lord wasn't after joiners. They're a dime a dozen. Americans are professional joiners. They'd die if they couldn't join something. Give them a red button and a certificate, and they'll join anything on the face of the earth. The Lord wasn't after joiners. He was after disciples.

Jesus said, "If any man come to me, and hate not his father, and mother, and wife, and children, and brethren, and sisters, yea, and his own life also, he cannot be my disciple. And whosoever doth not bear his cross, and come after me, cannot be my disciple" (Luke 14:26–27). He never put discipleship in fine print in the contract. He put it in boldface type clear across the page every time. Don't ever mistake it.

Paul said, "Who art thou, Lord? . . . Lord, what wilt thou have me to do?" (Acts 9:5–6). Two *Lords*; *Lord* came last in the first question and first in the second question. After you meet the Lord, He ought to always come first. Thomas, after the resurrection, said, "My Lord and my God" (John 20:28). John Wesley said a few mornings after Aldersgate, "I awoke with Jesus, master, in my heart and in my mouth." Charles Hadden Spurgeon, one of the greatest preachers of the past said, "If the convert declares that he knows the Lord's will but doesn't mean to attend to it, you're not to pamper his presumption. It is your duty to assure him that he is not saved. Do not imagine that the gospel is magnified or God glorified by telling them that they may be saved at this moment simply by accepting Christ as their Savior while they are wedded to their idols and their hearts are still in love with sin. If I do so, I tell them a lie; I pervert the gospel; I insult Christ and turn the grace of God into lasciviousness."

A. A. Hodge said, "Any man who thinks he is a Christian in that he has accepted Christ for justification when he did not at the same time accept Him for sanctification is miserably deluded in that very experience."

G. Campbell Morgan said, "I do not believe men are ever brought to a sense of their need of His saviorhood, save as they stand in the presence of His Lordship and discover their inability apart from regeneration to be obedient there to." I'm concerned today about the multitude of our church members who will take the saviorhood but not the sovereignty of my Lord. What good is pardon if we're going to live on in rebellion? What sort of business is this? I call it the rebellion of the redeemed. We say we're pardoned and then turn right around and say, "No, I will take Him as savior; I won't have Him as Lord." This is a contradiction. It's impossible.

Finally, the lordship of Christ will be the ultimate confession of creation, because we are told that the day is coming when at the name of Jesus every knee should bow in heaven, earth, and under the earth, and every tongue confess that Jesus Christ is Lord to the glory of God, the Father (Phil. 2:9–11). Don't ever ask a man, "Will you confess Christ as Lord?" Some day he will. You might wake him up if you say, "My friend, I'm not going to ask, 'Will you?' I'm just going to ask, 'When will you?'" You've got it to do. Will you do it now or when it is too late? Everybody has it to do. "Things in heaven, and things in earth, and things under the earth" (v. 10) takes in all the territory. That covers everywhere. This is not *universalism,* but it will be *universal.* Everybody will confess Christ's lordship, but it won't save the person who has waited out the opportunity.

Over in Scotland a young lady said to her pastor, "I think God wants me to be a missionary, and I don't want to be a missionary. What am I going to do?" He opened the New

Testament to Acts 10:14 where Peter had a little argument with the Lord, you remember, and said, "Not so, Lord." The pastor said, "Now look at that. That's a contradiction. If you say, 'Not so,' He's not Lord; if He's Lord, you just don't say 'not so.'" He said, "I'm going to leave this with you. I'm going out for a while. I want you to look at it, and I want you to pray about it. Then I want you to take a pencil and mark out either, 'not so' or 'Lord,' because you can't have both." When he returned she had marked out, 'not so,' and He was Lord.

Oh, what would happen today if we had churches filled with people with a one-word vocabulary, "Lord"? No strings, no reservations, just *Lord*. But so often, the lip confession is nullified by the life contradiction.

Is He your Lord?

ABOUT THE COMPILER AND EDITOR

Dennis J. Hester has pastored churches in North Carolina, South Carolina, and Virginia. He has also served as a chaplain, revivalist, and volunteer missionary. The author of numerous articles and newspaper columns, Dennis also has compiled three books on Vance Havner, *The Vance Havner Quotebook, The Vance Havner Notebook,* and *Sermon Sparklers by Vance Havner.* In addition to these titles, he is the author of *"Pastor, We Need to Talk!" How Congregations and Pastors Can Solve Their Problems Before It's Too Late.*

Dennis devotes much of his time to writing, speaking at and leading conferences, and consulting with churches in conflict and transition. He is a leader at workshops in communicating more effectively, managing and resolving conflict successfully, surviving and thriving through change, building and nurturing lasting relationships, and becoming leaders that others want to follow. You can learn more about Dennis and his ministry and subscribe to his online newsletter (e-zine) at www.betterchurches.com and dennishester@kregel.com. You can learn more about Vance Havner at www.vancehavnersermons.com.

Dennis and his wife Pam and their two children, Nathan and Rachael, make their home in Shelby, North Carolina.